Prayer of the HeART

Prayer of the HeART

a journey through the heART with visual prayer

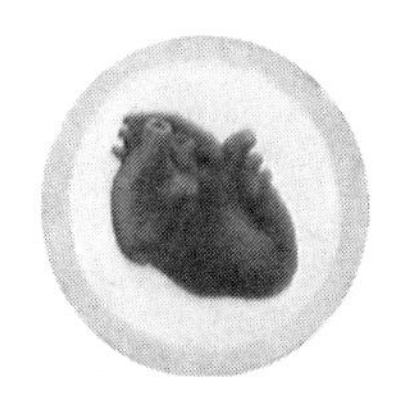

KELLY SCHNEIDER CONKLING

MOREHOUSE PUBLISHING
HARRISBURG • PENNSYLVANIA

Morehouse Publishing, P.O. Box 1321, Harrisburg, PA 17105

Morehouse Publishing, 445 Fifth Avenue, New York, NY 10016

Morehouse Publishing is an imprint of

Church Publishing Incorporated.

"Landscape ot the Heart" (cover, pages iv and 25; acrylic, 2003)
and "Prayer of the Heart" (page 1; oil on tin, 1990)
by Kelly Schneider Conkling.

Cover design by Laurie Klein Westhafer

Library of Congress Cataloging-in-Publication Data

Conkling, Kelly Schneider.
Prayer of the heart / Kelly Schneider Conkling.
p. cm.
Includes bibliographical references.
ISBN-13: 978-0-8192-2168-1 (pbk.)
1. Prayer—Christianity. 2. Spiritual life—Christianity. 3. Meditation.
4. Spirituality in art. 5. Christianity and art. I. Title.
BV210.3.C65 2006
248.3—dc22

2006005491

Printed in the United States of America

06 07 08 09 10 9 8 7 6 5 4 3 2 1

To Sara and Emily
with love and deepest respect

Contents

Acknowledgments

I am very thankful to the women in my visual prayer groups and workshops for sharing their prayers and stories. They have taught me much about prayer and the depths of the heart. Thanks to Carol Raven for her great support and encouragement. To Elizabeth, John, and Frannie of Viva Bookstore in San Antonio, I am forever grateful for the opportunity to offer my Prayer of the heART workshops. Thanks to Nancy Fitzgerald for her suggestion that I write this book and for her good critique and editorial insights. My sister, Stacy Dowdy, whose reading of the manuscript and great advice kept me going. To my beautiful daughters, Sara and Emily, for letting me tell our stories. And to my husband, Allan, who loves and believes in me even when I cannot.

explorefaith.org books: An Introduction

The book you hold in your hand says a lot about you. It reflects your yearning to forge a deep and meaningful relationship with God, to open yourself to the countless ways we can experience the holy, to embrace an image of the divine that frees your soul and fortifies your heart. It is a book published with the spiritual pilgrim in mind through a collaboration of Morehouse Publishing and the Web site explorefaith.org.

The pilgrim's path cannot be mapped beforehand. It moves toward the sacred with twists and turns unique to you alone. Explore faith.org books honor the truth that we all discover the holy through different doorways, at different points in our lives. These books offer tools for your travels—resources to help you follow your soul's purest longings. Although their approach will change, their purpose remains constant. Our hope is that they will help clear the way for you, providing fruitful avenues for experiencing God's unceasing devotion and perfect love.

www.explorefaith.org

Spiritual guidance for anyone seeking a path to God

A non-profit Web site aimed at anyone interested in exploring spiritual issues, explorefaith.org provides an open, non-judgmental, private place for exploring your faith and deepening your connection to the sacred. Material on the site is rich and varied, created to highlight the wisdom of diverse faith traditions, while at the same time expressing the conviction that through Jesus Christ we can experience the heart of God. Tools for meditating with music, art and poetry; essays about the spiritual meaning in popular books and first-run films; a daily devotional meditation; informative and challenging responses to questions we have all pondered; excerpts from publications with a spiritual message—all this and more is available online at explorefaith.org. As stated on the site's "Who We Are" page, explore faith.org is deeply committed to the ongoing spiritual formation of people of all ages and all backgrounds, living in countries around the world. The simple goal is to help visitors navigate their journey in faith by providing rich and varied material about God, faith and spirituality. That material focuses on a God of grace and compassion, whose chief characteristic is love.

You have the book, now try the Web site. Visit us at www.explore faith.org. With its emphasis on God's infinite grace and the importance of experiencing the sacred, its openness and respect for different denominations and religions, and its grounding in the love of God expressed through Christianity, explorefaith.org can become a valued part of your faith-formation and on-going spiritual practice.

— INTRODUCTION —

In 1991 I was working on my Masters Degree in Art. The topic of my thesis was Prayer in Two and Three Dimensional Art, in which I explored the relationship between art, prayer, and spirituality, a long-time interest of mine. In addition to the written thesis, I was also required to create twenty pieces of artwork that related to the topic. For several years I had kept a sketchbook journal in which I recorded works, ideas, and images, and I turned to this for the inspiration for my art.

As I created each piece of art, it seemed to take on a life of its own. I found myself responding to the pieces without trying to analyze what was happening. Choices about painting the image or making it from clay, the colors I chose, details that appeared, all came from somewhere deep inside me, beyond my conscious thought. I discovered through this process that prayer has a reality of its own. It is not just words that are spoken and somehow drift off, hopefully reaching God, but it has a reality that is almost tangible.

After finishing the artwork, I had to finish writing the thesis and relate the art I had created to the idea of art as prayer. As I began to write, I realized that what I had done in my work was to put my life in visual form; each piece represented a prayer of a particular time in my life. But more importantly, I discovered that the very act of creating these pieces had been prayer. Prayer in its simplest form: the opening of my heart, my small heart, to God's very great heart.

Over the years that followed, I continued to explore the use of art in this way—as a form of prayer. It was something I did for myself, not thinking it could be beneficial to others. One day I was talking about this with my friend Carol, who expressed an interest in learning the practice of visual prayer. We began to meet regularly to pray in images and I discovered, through this time together, that this form of prayer could indeed be effective for other people, too. A short time later, I was asked to lead a women's retreat and I decided to use visual prayer as the topic, knowing that there would be a large group of women with many different interests. I was fearful but expectant, not knowing what kind of response I would receive, but feeling that what I had to offer was important. It was very well received.

In 2004, I began to offer workshops on Prayer of the heART, as well as Spiritual Direction Groups that focused on the use of visual prayer. This book grew out of the workshops and insight gained from these workshops and from group direction, and I share what I have learned with you. In Part 1, I present a broad overview of the steps and techniques of visual prayers. In Part 2, I have given you detailed instructions to guide you through each visual prayer exercise.

I invite you to relax, open your heart, and enter into a journey which will lead you into the depths of your heart. There, in the words of W. H. Auden, you will find "rare beasts and have unique adventures."[1]

1. W. H. Auden, *He Is the Way* (New York: Church Hymnal Corporation, 1982), 464.

Part 1

Prayer of the heART

1

— HEART SPIRITUALITY —

Art. Images. Symbols. God. Life. Sacraments. Incarnation. These have always been intrinsically bound together for me. From an early age I saw and sought God through these means, even when I wasn't aware of what I was doing. Playing on the floor around the altar while my mother and grandmother worked—before I was big enough to help. Later, getting up early on Saturday morning to go out and cut flowers before the day got too hot. Placing them in deep water and taking them to the church to prepare them for the altar. Polishing the brass. Preparing the linens. Setting the altar. Placing the candles just right. Touching the rich purples, greens, reds, and whites of the hangings, soft, smooth, laced with golden threads and tassels. Watching the reflection of colors from the stained glass windows dance across the pews and the floor. Feeling the silence. Sensing the presence of God in that place and in and through the images and symbols all around me.

I am a visual person, somebody who experiences God best through the senses—touching, smelling, hearing, seeing, tasting, and the sacramental experiences of daily life, from flowers to a beautiful work of art, from a cup of tea with my mother to a walk with my husband to sitting on the patio listening to birdsong. Prayer is an integral part of these simple acts of living. It's an intentional awareness of God in, with, and through all aspects of our lives. And yet, at times prayer can be very elusive—words, ideas, thoughts, and conversations with God that seem to go nowhere, that have no sense of reality. For years I sought forms of prayer that had tangible elements to them. I looked and read and searched many places.

When I was about seven, my grandfather gave me a set of art books that covered the span of human artistic development in every culture. There were twelve books in all with hundreds of images of paintings, drawings, sculpture, and artifacts. I spent many an hour as I grew up looking through these books, over and over again, intrigued by the variety of expression. I remember being drawn in particular to the "religious" art work, both curious and confused by the artist's ability to represent God or the gods of their culture. I began to realize deep within my soul that there was a deep connection between God, art, and the stirrings of my heart.

My first conscious connection of prayer and art—tangible, visual prayer—came with my discovery of the Scottish minister and author George MacDonald. In his book, *Lilith*, an adult fairy tale, he writes of a man who is taken to a parallel world. As he and the raven, his guide, are walking through the church cemetery, the raven points out a flower—a prayer flower. After a discussion about how a flower could really be a prayer, the man states, "But I did see that the flower was different from any flower I had ever seen before; therefore I knew that I must be seeing a shadow of the prayer in it; and a great awe came over me to think of the heart listening to the flower."[1] The great Heart listening to one of its little hearts. This concept struck me like a bolt of lightening: The heart of God, in which we live and move and have our being, listens to the longings and groanings of our little hearts.

This is a book about prayer. It's a book about a method of prayer using visual images as the means through which we allow God to speak with us. Ranier Maria Rilke wrote, "Work of the eyes is done, begin heartwork now on those images in you, those captive ones."[2]

Our culture today is in dire need of doing "heartwork." In the Celtic tradition there's a clear sense of our having been created in the

---

1. George MacDonald, *Lilith* (Grand Rapids, Mich.: Eerdmans, 1981), 26.

2. Ranier Maria Rilke, "Turning," in Edward Snow, *Uncollected Poems: Ranier Maria Rilke* (New York: North Point Press, 1996), 91.

image and likeness of God and an embracing of all that entails: our innate goodness, our free will, and our responsibility to be co-creators with God in this world today. In what my now grown-up daughter calls our "generic" culture, I've found that visual imaging, used as prayer, can help with the "heartwork"—to find that center within ourselves where God dwells and in which we live and move and have our being.

Recovering an Ancient Way of Thinking

The great Heart listening to its little hearts. The heart of God listening to the hearts of God's children. When I was in seminary, I discovered an affirmation of this connection between the heart and prayer in the writings of a fifth-century Syrian mystic, Pseudo-Macarius. He wrote of our journey to God as a progression of the heart—a progression from a heart that was sinful, to a heart infused by grace, and finally to a heart that totally belonged to God. This heart spirituality of Macarius is based in the ancient Hebrew understanding of heart, which influenced all of the Old and New Testaments and continued for many centuries in the Christian Church.

One of the striking things about the Judeo-Christian concept of God is that our God is a God with a heart. In turn, this God of ours, in whose image we are created, has given us a heart. The ancient understanding of "heart" is one that is multi-dimensional. The heart is the place of our emotions and affections. It is the place of thinking and wisdom, the place where our free will and conscience reside. In this way, the heart specifically refers to the human person as a whole. The heart is the core of our being, our inner self, and, most importantly, it is the place where we come face to face with God. It is the place where the Spirit of God is active.

It is this rich understanding of the heart that Macarius had in mind when he attempted to explain the workings of the heart in relationship to prayer. He wrote:

> The heart itself is but a small vessel, yet dragons are there,
> and there are also lions; there are poisonous beasts
> and all the treasures of evil. There also are rough and uneven
> roads; there are precipices. But there too is God, the angels,

the life and the Kingdom, the light and the apostles
the heavenly cities and the treasures of grace—all things are there.[3]

During the 1990s I saw a movie called *Restoration*. Set in England during the seventeenth century, it was about the life of a doctor. In one memorable scene, the doctor and his friend see a man who had come to the hospital with a kind of leather shield over his chest. They gather around, and he unbuckles the shield opening the front flap. Beneath the shield his chest is open—open and red like a wound, but open as if it had grown that way, with his beating heart clearly visible. The doctor and his friend, of course, are amazed. The man with the open chest asks if the friend wants to touch his heart. Enthralled and fascinated, he's also afraid and can not bring himself to. The man then invites the doctor, who slowly steps up and tentatively reaches out to touch the heart; a smile of joy, amazement, and understanding spreading over his face at the moment of contact.

In the seventeenth century, William Harvey, an English doctor, actually did present to his colleagues at the Royal College of Physicians a visible, tangible heart, one that could be held in the hand, measured, and dissected.[4] At this moment, the heart became "demythologized." As James Hillman wrote in *The Thought of the Heart and the Soul of the World*, "Thought lost its heart, heart its thought."[5] Human beings' love affair with scientific proof pushed away the heart of the past. Emphasis was placed on the "real" heart rather than the "symbolic" heart. Now when the heart was spoken of, it was the physical muscle in the breast. Any ancient understanding was relegated to metaphorical sayings like "wearing his heart on his sleeve." From this point on,

3. George A. Maloney, S.J., ed., *Pseudo-Macarius: The Fifty Spiritual Homilies and The Great Letter* (New York: Paulist Press, 1992), 222.

4. Gail Godwin, *Heart: A Natural History of the Heart-Filled Life* (New York: Perrenial, 2002), 112.

5. James Hillman, quoted in ibid., 113.

the divide between heart and mind, heart and emotions, has continued to grow.

The heart is literally a muscle, an organ in our body, which pumps blood. But is that all there is to the heart, or were the ancient Hebrews on to something? Today we are now beginning to see that this "pump in the chest" isn't all there is to it. Recently scientists in the field of neurocardiology have discovered that the heart has its own nervous system that functions independently from the brain. Simply stated, it receives and sends information to the brain that creates a two-way communication between the two organs.[6] The heart and brain "talk" to each other. The heart sends feelings and emotions to the brain, which in turn affect our health and well-being. So the metaphor of the heart by Macarius is really quite accurate. As we begin to recover an old way of looking at the "seat of our emotions," we find that there are deeper levels of "truth" than there are in cold, rational biology alone. "The heart, as the innermost spring of human personality is directly open to God and subject to his influence."[7] Indeed, as we read in Psalm 33:15, God "fashions the hearts of them all."

In seeking to recover Heart Spirituality, we're connecting ourselves to the very core of our being. It's the path, the way, which Jesus taught—a way of living into and existing within the heart of God. As Meister Eckhart said of God, "You don't need to seek him here or there. He is not farther off than the door of your heart."[8] In the process of visual prayer and journaling, which focuses on heart spirituality, we can learn a lot about the landscape of our own hearts as Macarius described them, discover deeper truths about ourselves, and make contact with God through ancient ways of prayer, journaling, and art, seeing and exploring them in new ways.

---

6. *The Inside Story: Understanding the Power of Feelings* (Boulder Creek, Calif.: Institute of HeartMath, 2002), 23.

7. *The Interpreter's Dictionary of the Bible, Vol. E–J* (New York: Abingdon Press, 1962), 550.

8. Meister Eckhart, *Breakthrough: Meister Eckhart's Creation Spirituality in New Translation* (New York: Doubleday, 1980), 242.

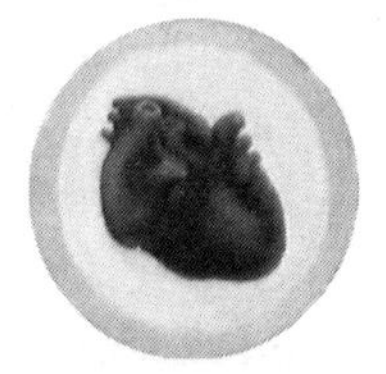

2

— HEART AS PRAYER —

It was late in the evening. It had been one of those days—the kind of day when you find yourself anxiously awaiting the moment you get all of your work and chores done and can finally get to bed for a good rest. And that moment finally came—at last. Emily seemed to be asleep—her little three-year-old noises and singing stopped after several hours of struggling to avoid sleep. I listened once more, just in case. All was quiet. I put my book down, settled my pillows, turned off the light.

"Mommy!"

Oh, Lord, I thought. What is it now? Surely I didn't hear that. It's just my imagination. I turned over.

"Mommeeee!" This time I couldn't deny it. A voice was coming from the other room. Not Emily, but Sara. Sara, unlike her little sister, had always been a good sleeper and seldom woke up in the night. So what's wrong?

"Maaaa-m!" This time louder and more insistent.

As I began to pull myself up and out of bed, I went over the list of possibilities in my mind: Sick? She seemed okay earlier. Bathroom? Not usually the case. Thirsty? Maybe. Bad dream? Probably.

I went into Sara's room to see what was wrong, what she needed, hoping that it wouldn't be too involved.

"What is it? What's wrong?" I asked as I walked up to her bedside. "Are you okay?"

"Do you have God's address?" she asked, very simply. Not at all what I expected.

"God's address?" I asked kind of stupidly, trying to wake up enough to talk with her.

"Yes. God's address. I need it."

Okay, I thought. This isn't going to be a simple glass of water. I sat down beside her on the bed and began to explain, as best I could, that God didn't have an address like we do and that when we want to talk with God we use prayer. I then proceeded to try to explain prayer to her when she interrupted.

"Mother. I know all that," she said, rather put out with me. "But I pray and pray and I never get an answer. So I want to get God's address so I can write him a letter and he can send me a letter back!"

Oh, Sara, I thought. So do I.

My concept of prayer is really quite simple. For me, prayer is the longing of the heart, the desire to feel whole, to be in touch with myself, the universe, and most importantly, God. Any feeling that truly comes from the heart is prayer—an expression of myself reaching out for a sympathetic, loving presence. Even those feelings which I may think are "unholy," feelings of hate, envy, lust, when directed God-ward, as the psalmists did, are prayer. The Psalms are filled a myriad of emotions: fear, joy, hatred, anger, exaltation, all openly and honestly held up to God. The Psalm I find most disturbing is Psalm 137, which ends with this verse: "Happy shall they be who take your little ones and dash them against the rock!" Yet even this, as incomprehensible as it is for me, is the psalmist's prayer because it's an honest expression of feelings. To hold these kinds of feeling in, thinking that they are not "holy" enough to present to God, is to keep ourselves from a true and full relationship with God. Getting them out, on the other hand, allows us to turn them over to God for healing.

I have difficulty with words: keeping a journal or even praying in words. As much as I try, the words always sound a bit empty, false, never truly conveying what I really mean or how I really feel. I know what the Apostle Paul means when he writes, "Likewise the Spirit helps us in our weakness; for we do not know how to pray as we ought, but that very Spirit intercedes with sighs too deep for words. And God, who searches the heart, knows what is the mind of the Spirit, because the Spirit intercedes for the saints according to the will of God" (Romans 8:26–27).

Words describe, images express. By using a combination of centering, imaging, and words I've found I can communicate with and discern God's will at a much deeper level. This process is very much like dreaming on paper. It is visual prayer.

Visual prayer is the opening of our heart to God—allowing the Holy Spirit to speak through the images we place on paper. It's fully open-hearted—not closed and controlled. There's so much we can learn through this process of prayer, which connects with the "spirituality of the heart" of Macarius.[1]

If then we embark upon that progression to God, it stands to reason that there are many ways to travel that journey. Visual prayer is one path. It is not meant to be our primary form of prayer, but an addition to it. An increased awareness of the visual can give God another way to speak to us and gives us another way to respond. Art and prayer both involve trusting a process. What they share in common is that we don't know what is going to happen until we begin. You cannot control the outcome. Getting started is the hardest part. And just like traditional prayer disciplines, you will not get comfortable with it until you practice it.

This book is not about "art" in the sense of creating splendid pictures. Nor is it only for professionally trained artists. You don't need to be an artist to create visual images directed by the Holy Spirit. So if you don't think of yourself as an artist, relax. This isn't about creating

1. George A. Maloney, S.J., ed., *Pseudo-Macarius: The Fifty Spiritual Homilies and The Great Letter* (New York: Paulist Press, 1992), xiii.

"works of art," but about doing "art work"—the work of the heart in images. In fact, you have an advantage over those who are trained artists. I've found that artists who have a very difficult time letting go of their need for a particular result don't always get the most benefit out of this form of prayer. As an amateur, you may have an easier time letting go of your need for a desired outcome and letting yourself be directed totally by the prompting of the Spirit.

George MacDonald wrote of "the groaning [of the heart] that cannot be uttered." Perhaps, he suggested, that's just what music (art) is meant for—to say the things that are shapeless and wordless, yet are also intensely alive.[2] Art as prayer is communication and expression in the form of a visual metaphor with the intention of opening our heart and mind toward God. It is not so much the expression of an experience of God, rather it is the visual result of an experience *with and through* God. Visual imaging, art as prayer, invites God to be the director, writer, and artist of our hearts, and the result is a visual, tangible, "letter" from God.

---

2. George MacDonald, *The Shopkeeper's Daughter* (Wheaton, Ill.: Victor Books, 1986), 212.

3

— VISUAL PRAYER AND JOURNALING —

Visual prayer with journaling uses a combination of visual journaling and art therapy techniques balanced by spiritual discernment, reflection, and meditation. While visual prayer uses art therapy techniques, it's not the same thing. It's the intention that makes it different. In art therapy, the focus is on the individual psychological state and discernment is focused on what the images reveal psychologically, while the spiritual isn't necessarily considered. But using these imaging techniques as prayer for spiritual discernment allows for both—though the process may very well yield some psychological insight, the focus is on the spiritual. You can take the spiritual out of the psychological but you can't take the psychological out of the spiritual—they inform each other. In visual prayer, both the psychological and spiritual interact to provide a deeper dialogue with God.

The goal of visual prayer and journaling isn't only to delve into the depths of our hearts to discover our true selves, but—more importantly—to find God and nurture the love relationship God always intended. In Ephesians, Paul asks that God strengthen us in our inner being through his Spirit and that Christ may dwell in our hearts. And in Romans and Galatians, Paul talks of the Spirit dwelling within our hearts and being active in our lives. In our Judeo-Christian tradition, the heart is the core of our being, the place where we can discover our true nature. It's also the place where we come face to face with God, and where the Holy Spirit is active. It's the place where there's a tangible awareness of God's presence and grace. Surveying the landscape of our hearts is a way of finding ourselves and our God.

Materials

The materials you need to begin are really very simple: a sketch book with blank pages, a box of twenty-four crayons or oil pastels, and a pencil or pen.

For your sketchbook, I suggest an unlined 11x14-inch spiral. This size gives you some versatility and the spiral allows you to open your book flat when drawing or journaling. As you progress, you may want to work with something larger. I've found that there are times when the prayer needs more space and a larger piece of paper gives me the freedom to express, both visually and physically. For large images that aren't bound in your sketch book, an inexpensive portfolio is a good way to store your images. You may also want a smaller sketchbook—a 4x6-inch journal, for example, that you can carry with you when you travel or use at free moments during the day. One teacher who uses this prayer technique keeps her small journal with her at work so that if things get too stressful, she can pray her visual prayer to help her re-center. Others like the smaller journals because they're more comfortable working on a smaller field. Experiment to find the size that suits you best.

Crayons and oil pastels are best to begin with because they're simple, not messy, and portable. But feel free to try any other art materials you like. I've found that colored pencils are much slower to use and don't allow for the immediacy of expression in prayer time. Water colors are great to use if you have the space and the appropriate paper. Dry pastels are great, too, if you've got a separate workspace where dust won't be a problem.

Creating Sacred Space

The word "sacred" comes from the Greek *saos*, which means "safe," and from the Latin *sacre*, which means "to set apart" or "make holy," to dedicate to some particular person or purpose by which it is not to be profaned, violated, or made common.[1] A sacred space is a place in which we feel safe, nurtured, and centered mentally, physically, emotionally, and spiritually. It's a place where we can safely explore our deepest thoughts and feelings. It's a place set apart for God, where we can open our hearts to God. It should be a place of quiet and beauty, free from interruptions.

If you don't already have a sacred space where you pray regularly, think about finding one. It can be anywhere you choose to set aside for yourself. You may have to improvise, so look around your home and be creative. One woman I know has set up her sacred space in her laundry room—no one bothers her in there. Another chose her bathroom—the house rule is not to bother Mom in the bathroom so that room was a natural for privacy and quiet.

It's helpful to have a table where you can spread your colors out before you, as keeping them in the box limits the immediacy of expression. Find a container—a basket is a good choice—to keep your visual prayer journal and materials all the time so that you don't have to go looking for them each time

Fill your special space with flowers, candles, icons, family pictures, a cross, incense—whatever makes it holy and welcoming and beautiful for you. Quiet music is helpful for some people too.

Of course, you can venture out to work in other places, too. I like to work outside on my patio in nice weather, and I always carry a small journal and crayons with me just in case the need arises. But make your special sacred place a part of your regular prayer time, set apart and dedicated to God.

Basic Steps in Visual Prayer

There are three basic techniques of visual prayer: expressive drawing, the mandala, the scribble drawing. While each of these is unique, all three visual prayer processes follow the same basic steps.[2] In order to

---

1. *Webster's New Twentieth Century Dictionary Unabridged*, 2nd Ed. (New York: Simon and Schuster, 1972), 1593.

2. For other information regarding basic visual journaling steps, I recommend reading Barbara Ganim and Susan Fox's *Visual Journaling: Going Deeper than Words* (Wheaton, Ill.: Quest Books, 1999).

give you a sense of what is involved, I am giving you a broad overview of each step at this time. In Part 2 you will be given detailed instructions for each exercise.

1. **Preparing**: Lay your prayer journal or drawing pad out before you, open to the blank page on which you intend to draw. If you're drawing in your journal and you're right handed, try drawing on the back of the first blank left-hand page, and journal on the opposite right-hand page. If you're left handed, do the opposite. (See fig. 1.) This will allow you to easily see your visual prayer on one page while dialoguing with the image on the opposite page. If you're using a large drawing pad, have your prayer journal open to a blank page so you can dialogue with your image in your journal. Keep your drawing materials—crayons, oil pastels, and so on—within easy reach.

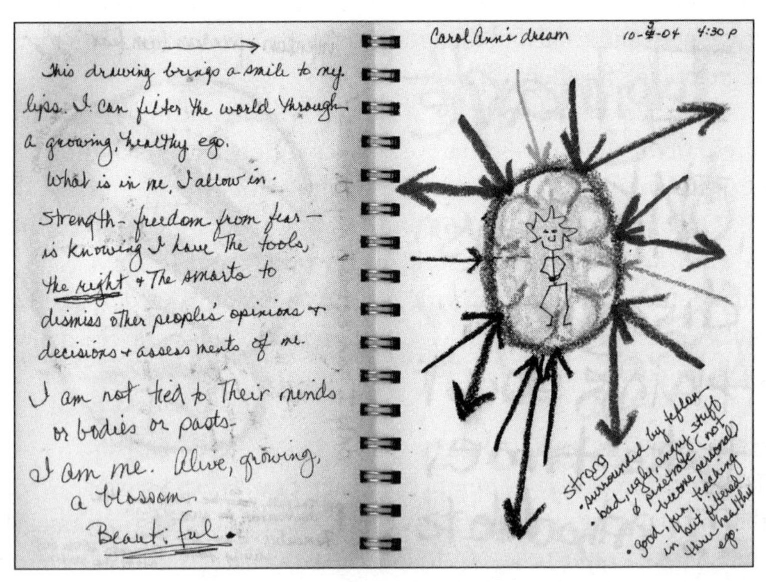

Fig. 1. Left-handed journal entry by Carol R.

2. **Focusing the heart**: In this step, center yourself and your heart on God. If you've ever practiced centering prayer, you'll be familiar with parts of this step. Begin by focusing on your body and whatever thoughts or concerns you have for the day, and let then

letting them go. (A detailed guide for centering will be presented in the prayer exercises to follow.) When you feel relaxed, decide on your prayer focus. Since intention is important in visual prayer, it's helpful to have a focus that reflects what's on your mind, how you're feeling, or what you want to talk with God about. In this form of prayer, you're not asking God for something. You're opening your heart to hear what God has to say to you.

The visual prayer image that results from the prayer time is usually related to your prayer focus. But God might respond in very unexpected ways. Sometimes a prayer focus takes several images to work itself out, and sometimes it may take months of dialoguing with the images. Issues of forgiveness are an example of a prayer focus that, because of the intensity of the feelings and need, will probably take more than one prayer session to work out. So try not to rush. Examples of a prayer focus are:

- God, what do you have to say to me today?
- God, I'm feeling frustrated with all the work I have to do today. Help me to find your presence in the day ahead.
- I'm so angry with Joan, God. Help me see what I need to do in this situation.
- God, this has been such an incredible day. I thank you for the blessings it has brought me.

You can be as specific as you need to be. Remember, it's okay to hold up anything you're feeling or thinking to God in prayer.

Once you've found your prayer focus, write it down in your journal. At this point you'll begin the process of opening yourself to the Spirit, letting go of your control and needs, and asking God to open your heart and guide you. Remain in this step as long as you need to. You'll know when you feel connected to God and are ready to begin. At this point, you will offer your prayer to God. Continue centering until you feel God nudging you to begin.

3. **Prayer of the heart**: Decide which of the three prayer techniques you feel God is leading you to use. Let go and allow the Spirit to draw your image. You won't be deciding what you draw or what colors to use. You're opening yourself instead to the guidance of

the Spirit. If you find that you're analyzing what you're doing, trying to control the colors or images, or being critical of what you see, stop immediately, apologize to God for interrupting, re-center, and then continue. Stay in this step until you feel finished.

4. **Listening to the image**: Now you'll dialogue with God through the image. It's like reading God's letter to you.

   First, you can let the experience be enough, and simply title and date your image, noting your initial response and feelings. This may be all that you need to do and it may well be enough. You can go back to the image later and do some deeper analysis.

   Second, you can take this a step further by working through basic questions that will allow you to look deeper into the image. It's really quite simple, and you can always choose how deeply you want to dialogue—there are many layers to analyzing or dialoguing with God through your image. You may want to go to a deeper level of dialogue by journaling on the feelings and color symbolism. In each exercise in Part 2, I have provided questions to help with this type of dialogue. I encourage you to do this because it is in the dialogue that you can discover a deeper experience with God. You can also go even deeper by looking at the other symbols in the image: numbers, shapes, recognizable images, the relationship between these, and so on. Whatever level of dialogue you choose, from looking strictly at the surface level to looking into the deeper symbolism, you'll discover things that you may not have been aware of.

A few things to remember in this step of listening:

1. Always go back to your prayer focus when dialoguing with the image and seeking to see what God may be saying to you or how God may be directing you. Sometimes you'll be surprised by what you see, sometimes your image will affirm what you already know, and sometimes you'll be disturbed and troubled with more questions than you began with. If that happens to you, use these questions as the focus of your next prayer.

2. Look back and note how you were feeling as you were drawing—and even note the way you were drawing. Were you feeling agitated, drawing your lines hard and fast, with great intensity? Or were you feeling a sense of peace, putting down lines and colors slowly and softly, like a caress?

After finishing a prayer, I like to leave the image out somewhere during the day so I can see it and be reminded of my time with God. Often I'll go back and continue the dialogue with the image, especially if I didn't feel I'd explored it enough, or if I wasn't ready to listen very deeply.

Three Visual Prayer Techniques

Now that you have a sense of the basic steps involved in visual prayer, I want to give you an overview of the three visual prayer techniques that we'll use in the exercises in Part 2. These are simple descriptions of the process involved in each technique, not complete instructions in the prayer process. Detailed guidelines will be presented with each exercise in Part 2 to guide you through the three techniques

As you practice the prayers in Part 2, know that you are not limited by these techniques. While each exercise focuses on one prayer technique, any of the techniques will work well. You may try any of them at any time. As you become more comfortable with visual prayer, you'll find a favorite technique that you use most of the time. That's fine—but don't limit yourself to just that one. I've found there are times when I'm led to one or the other of the three. I encourage you to be open to the nudging of the Spirit before determining which technique to use. You'll also find that you'll develop your own visual language as you begin to recognize colors and symbols that you can interpret and read easily.

Expressive Prayer

Expressive drawing is a very basic technique of accessing the subconscious. After centering on God and holding up your prayer focus, select a color your heart guides you to, and then, allowing the Spirit to direct you, draw whatever comes to you. It may be only random lines, shapes, and colors, like an expressionist drawing. Or you may find yourself including recognizable images like a tree, a flower, or a boat.

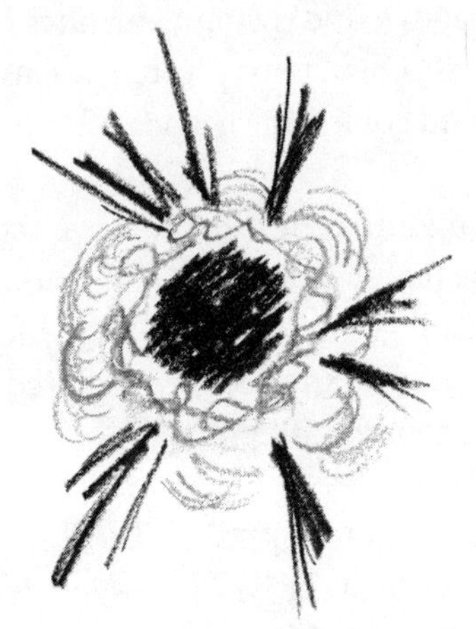

Fig. 2. Expressive prayer with abstract images.

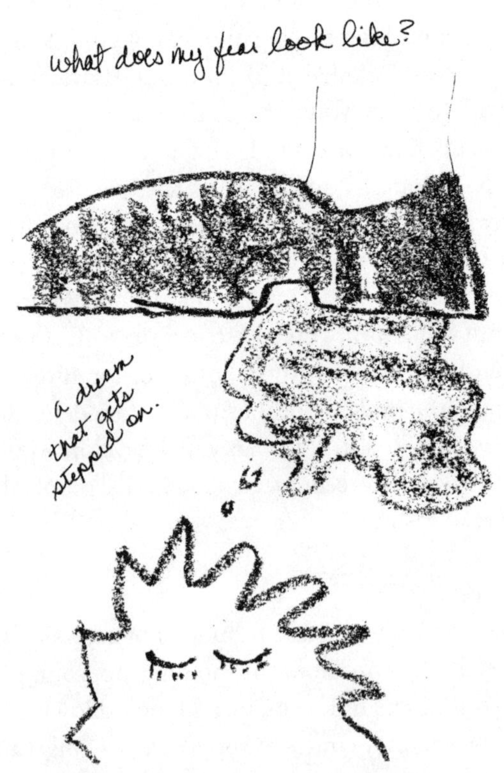

Fig. 3. Expressive prayer with recognizable images.

Scribble Prayer

The scribble is an excellent way to allow God to speak. It's very intuitive and open-ended. The process involves randomly scribbling over the page, with eyes closed, and then seeing what images are brought to mind when you look at it, like finding images in the clouds. Once you find an image, you'll complete it as God directs by adding details to bring it to life. Sometimes you'll stay within the scribble lines, but often you'll find yourself ignoring the scribble lines to complete the image (see Fig. 4 and 5).

Fig. 4. Scribble prayer staying within scribble lines by Brigid.

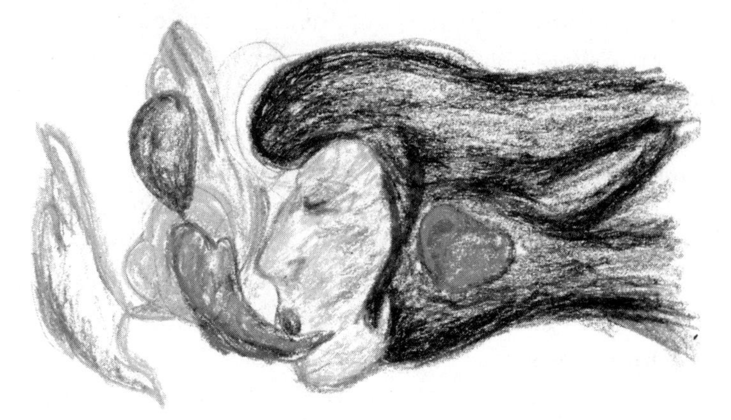

Fig. 5. Scribble prayer going beyond scribble lines.

Praying the Mandala

The mandala is probably the most well-known of the prayer forms presented here. Mandala is the Sanskrit word for "circle," or center. Circle drawings are an archetypal symbol found in cultures all over the world: ancient rock carvings in Africa, Europe, and North America, in Hindu and Tibetan Buddhist rituals, in Native American sand painting, and Celtic imagery, to name only a few. Hildegard of Bingen, a twelfth-century Benedictine nun, used the mandala form in drawing some of her visions. In modern times, Carl Jung brought the mandala into use for psychotherapy. In his use of mandalas, both personally and with clients, he came to associate them with the Self, the center of the total personality. The drawing of mandalas is now used by art therapists and many individuals as a means of personal insight and healing.

The mandala lends itself well as a form of prayer. The circle itself is balancing, calming, and centering. Drawing the circle creates a sacred space within which to pray. After you've drawn the circle, you'll add images, either recognizable or abstract. Many people find this prayer form the one they're drawn to practice most often.

One example of the versatility of the mandala is an experience one woman in my spiritual direction groups had. She had been having trouble using the scribble drawing as a prayer form. Her life had been very difficult and chaotic, both in the past and in the present, and the process of visual prayer had brought up many difficult things for her. She felt led to do a scribble prayer, but was afraid, feeling it was too open-ended with no way of exercising control. One evening, as she was centering and preparing to pray another mandala, she found herself, after having drawn the initial circle, scribbling inside the circle. By combining the two prayer forms, she found a new freedom and deep insight from God. For her, the circle of the mandala created a "safe space" within which to work—even scribble.

The circle also sets boundaries. You can stay within the boundary of the circle or venture outside. Emma, who admits she likes boundaries and is uncomfortable going outside of her limits, was excited when her prayer extended outside the boundary of her circle. She felt as though God had given her permission to have the freedom to explore areas of her life that she'd been afraid of before. On the other hand, Cheryl, who has a problem staying within boundaries in her personal life, found that in praying with the mandala, she felt that she must stay within the boundary of the circle. This allowed her to feel safe and in control. Either approach—staying in the boundary or going outside the circle—says something about where you are on your journey and where you need to go (see Fig. 6 and 7).

Fig. 6. Prayer staying within the boundary of the circle.

Fig. 7. Mandala prayer extending beyond the boundary.

Obstacles and Questions

The biggest obstacle to this type of prayer is fear. Fear that you're not good enough at drawing. Fear that you aren't doing it right. Fear that you won't be able to understand what God is saying in the images. Those old songs start playing in your head, telling you that "you can't draw," or "you're not coloring inside the lines," or any other of a number of things that your past experiences with art have told you.

If you're an artist, you may fear letting go of the need to control the outcome. Anna, a professional artist, had a very hard time with this at first. She knew how to follow her creative urgings, but she also knew how to balance this with her training and experience to create an aesthetically pleasing piece. After having prayed her first visual prayer using the mandala, she stood up to present it to the group. She said, "This is so humbling, and I am so embarrassed. This looks like a complete mess. It's all scribbles and there's nothing pleasing about it all. I don't work this way." She began to cry as she continued. "But it's all here." She'd lost a child many years earlier and had thought she'd dealt with her grief and sense of loss and put it behind her. In the process of prayer, God allowed her to see that it indeed wasn't behind her but was an integral part of who she was. She journaled on this image for quite a while, and it led her to questions she used as prayer focuses to follow.

If you don't think of yourself as an artist you may fear doing it "wrong." Georgia asked, "How do I know that God is directing what I do and not me? I pick colors, I draw things, but I'm not sure that it's God and not me." But I told Georgia—and I offer to you—the words of Erasmus made popular by Carl Jung: "Bidden or unbidden, God is present." Do your best. When you begin to question yourself, stop and re-center. God is present no matter what, and you will always receive something of benefit from the prayer time.

Part 2

Journey to the heART

The heart itself is but a small vessel, yet dragons are there,
and there are also lions; there are poisonous beasts
and all the treasures of evil. There also are rough and uneven
roads; there are precipices. But there too is God, the angels,
the life and the Kingdom, the light and the apostles
the heavenly cities and the treasures of grace—all things
are there.

— Pseudo-Macarius, *The Fifty Spiritual Homilies and The Great Letter*, edited by George Maloney (New York: Paulist Press, 1992).

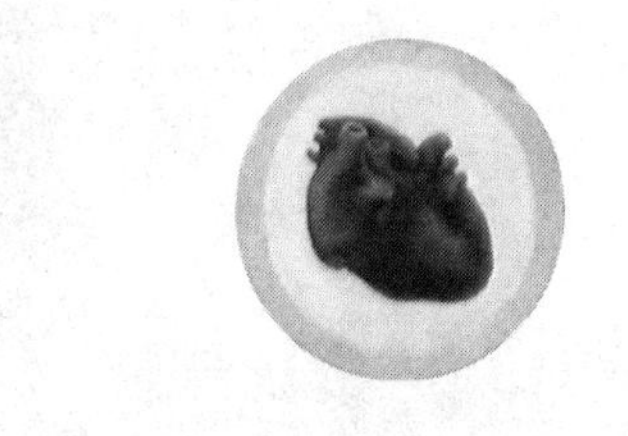

4

— THE heART ITSELF IS BUT A SMALL VESSEL —

Surveying the Landscape of the heART

I remember well the first time I was aware of God's creative force in the shaping of my life; the quiet evening I experienced the act of creativity as prayer. I'd been divorced for a year, with daughters two and four years old, and was struggling to keep my gift and interior shop open. I'd put the girls to bed and was sitting in my grandmother's old chartreuse plastic stuffed recliner, feeling anxious, unsettled, and a little depressed. Apart from my struggle to keep my business solvent, I had no sense of direction other than taking care of my girls—keeping food on the table and a roof over our heads.

That night, the living room was dark, with a couple of candles giving off their soft light. As I sat there, I felt a new sense of restlessness in my spirit, one I did not recognize, and I was unsure where it was coming from. Sitting on the table beside me was a big, deep-red zinnia—or more accurately, just the top of one. My daughter Sara had picked it for me earlier in the day and, in the manner of most small children, she had picked only the head—no stem. I looked at the zinnia floating on the top of a glass of water, and suddenly had the great desire to draw it. Why?

I was startled by the strength and urgency of my feelings. Even though I had a degree in art, I'd stopped working about six or so years before. It was too painful, too hard. I had no confidence in myself or my abilities; my love for art seemed to have dried up with my marriage. I no longer even made an attempt to draw, not even to make a simple sketch. So I found myself, quite surprisingly, sitting with this big, red zinnia staring at me, calling to my heart to draw. "What do you want from me?" I angrily asked the flower. "What makes you think I could draw you even if I wanted to?" I found myself holding a conversation with the zinnia, and then with myself, arguing that I hadn't drawn in years and so I couldn't possibly draw now. But the zinnia wouldn't stop staring at me. I ignored it, but the growing desire to pick up a pencil and draw continued until I finally told myself, "If I do decide to try and draw, there's no one here to see; I don't have to worry about the final outcome, how bad it will be, how miserably I'll fail."

I found myself looking around the room as if to see if anyone was looking—a silly thought since I was alone and the girls were in bed. And somehow I realized that I *could* draw the zinnia. No one would ever know. No one would ever have to see it. "I'll just do it as quickly as I can," I thought. "I'll get it out of my system and then go to bed."

I unearthed a drawing pencil and some paper and sat back down in the chartreuse chair. I thought I'd only draw for a few minutes—make the attempt, put down the pencil, throw away the paper, and go to bed. But instead, time seemed to stop, and I felt God acting in my life, animating my pencil. Everything else seemed to fade away, and all my perceptions blended and crossed over into one another. The only thing I was aware of was the present moment.

At times like these—liminal moments—God can truly work within and through us to reach our innermost self, our hearts. That long-ago night, I was totally caught up in what I was seeing—the intricacy of the center of the flower with its tiny little yellow buds circling its deep brown heart; each red petal, unique and individual as it overlapped and played against its neighbors. I don't remember drawing, and I haven't a clue how much time passed by. But suddenly I was finished. I sat for a long time looking at the image I'd drawn, awed by what I saw; my hand had responded to what I saw and I was not even aware of it. I was only aware of the presence of God. My agitation and frustration were gone. I was at peace, with a new sense of excitement and hope growing within me.

In the words of George MacDonald, I'd opened my little heart to God's big heart in prayer, and God had responded and begun something new in me. For in the course of my marriage, I'd lost an important part of me, and God was bringing it back to life. I can't say I immediately began to draw and paint all the time or that all my feelings of inadequacy and doubt were gone. But I do know this: In that moment of drawing—that liminal time of being in God's presence and allowing God to speak to me through the creating of the image of the zinnia—I began to heal. I began to make a new start.

Each of us is born as a seed, full of the potential and possibilities to become all that God created us to be. Even so, the way we see ourselves and how we feel about ourselves, how we react to those around us, are all formed by the outside world. From the moment of our birth, from the moment we were held in the loving arms of our parents, or cared for by doctors and nurses, our sense of identity, our sense of self began to be formed by others: *What a beautiful baby! Oh, your baby—is it a boy or girl? What a good baby. What a fussy child. He does everything he's told. She's so smart. He never seems to want to play with the other kids no matter what I do. So smart. Always in trouble. Moody. Good natured. Responsible. Irresponsible.* We're created with an innate, God-given nature. But often the God-self—that true self, that self created in the image and likeness of God—somehow gets lost in everybody else's expectations and our own struggle to make sense of the world and our place in it. We spend our lives trying to "find" ourselves, to discover who God truly intends us to be, and what God wants for our lives. But I've found that the place to discover my true self—my God-self—is within the depths of my heart. In Psalm 64, the psalmist tells us that the heart is deep and so the whole person, who we truly are, is a mystery until we begin to survey the landscape of our hearts and discover all that is held within us. Visual prayer and journaling are ways to begin that survey.

The heart is such a complex organ, and it's hard to know where or how to begin to look deep within ourselves. That is why I love this quote from Macarius so very much; it gives me a palpable image of my heart:

> The heart itself is but a small vessel, yet dragons are there, and there are also lions; there are poisonous beasts and all the treasures of evil. There also are rough and uneven roads; there are precipices. But there too is God, the angels, the life and the Kingdom, the light and the apostles, the heavenly cities and the treasures of grace—all things are there.[1]

The heart is small but deep, and its landscape is varied and full of strange and wonderful things. It's also full of very frightening things we'd rather not know about ourselves. In surveying our hearts, some days the discovery is small and seemingly insignificant. Some days the discovery is life-changing. You'll always discover something, even if it's only an affirmation of what you already know.

Evelyn, a lovely woman in one of my journaling groups, shared with us her realization that "the heart does not lie." She laughed when she told us that when writing down this revelation in her journal, she inadvertently wrote "the art does not lie." Both statements are true. When you're true to the prayer process of image making, you'll come one step closer to yourself and to God. The challenge is to let go of your own ego and control needs, and allow God to help you explore the terrain of your heart, to allow God to be your guide.

In drawing the zinnia, God started me on the journey of exploration, very simply, very gently. I began to discover in myself things known and things unknown, things welcome and things unwelcome, things joyous and things sorrowful. All had combined to mold me into the person God wants me to be. The process continues each day; the difference is that now I am intentional about it. I present myself to God, blank paper and crayons in hand, and wait for God to illumine for me the next area of my heart's landscape that I am to begin to know and explore.

---

1. George A. Maloney, S. J., ed., *Pseudo-Macarius: The Fifty Homilies and The Great Letter* (New York: Paulist Press, 1992), 222.

Beginning the Journey of Exploration

Exercise One—Expressive Prayer

In the visual journaling process, like most everything else, the hardest part is beginning. A blank piece of paper can be a scary thing, an intimidating space, and many doubts raise their ugly heads: I can't draw, how can I even attempt this? What if I can't draw what I see? What if God doesn't show me anything? What if it's me rather than God directing the drawing—how can I know? What if I can only scribble? These are common doubts, so please accept them, ignore them, and go on.

This simple exercise is a good way to pray with visual images, and it will also allow you to experiment with the image-making process.

Preparing and Focusing the heART

Turn your journal to the first blank double page and run your hands over the entire surface, noting the texture, the space, the edges. Whether you've decided to use regular crayons or oil pastels, take them out of the box and lay them out on the table before you. At the top of the blank page on the right of your journal, write the date and your prayer focus: "God, help me get in touch with how I am feeling today." Now set your journal down and sit back quietly.

Close your eyes and take deep, even breaths. This process is one of progression, beginning with the outward world around you, drawing inward to concentrate on yourself and how you are, and finally focusing even deeper—on God. Take note of your surroundings, the sounds, the thoughts in your mind and breathe easily and deeply, accepting the world around you as it is at this moment.

Next, focus on your body and how it feels. Notice your breathing. If you are feeling any discomfort—back pain, upset stomach, headache—note how it feels. Now focus on your heart, feel your heartbeat, and note how your heart feels—sad, anxious, stressed, contented? Can you imagine your heart in your mind's eye?

As you begin to feel that you are in touch with yourself, change your focus to God and ask for an awareness of God's presence within and around you. Ask God to send the Holy Spirit into your heart to speak through images you will receive. When you feel a connection with God, keep your eyes closed and ask God to help you "see" how you are feeling. What does your body, your heart, tell you? Consider what you feel and imagine what this feeling would look like if it were an image. What colors, shapes, or forms would best express it? You may actually see a recognizable image, or you may only sense a likeness, a vague awareness of something. Continue to keep your eyes closed, breathing deeply and evenly until you feel ready. Don't rush it—you will sense when you are ready.

Prayer of the heART

Open your eyes, and begin to draw your image, but don't worry if you didn't "see" or imagine anything; ask God to direct you. My friend Carol said of this point in the process, "I'm falling in love with the blank page. The circle or scribble connects my heart to the page. Going on from there seems natural, if not easy." So pick up whatever color jumps out at you, whatever color your eye is drawn to, even if you don't like it or wouldn't normally use it. Remember, you are allowing God to draw the image *through* you, so you shouldn't try to control the choice of colors or images that appear. Allow your hand to move any way that expresses your feelings, whether the outcome is a tree, a simple stick figure, a flower, the sun, or just scribbles, shapes, blobs, and lines. If you feel that you are taking over, are questioning too much, or are concerned over what you're doing or how it looks, put the crayon down, close your eyes, and refocus on God.

Listening to the Image

When you feel finished, put your colors down and thank God for the gift of this image. Under your written prayer focus, write down your first impression of your drawing. It may be one word like "stressed" or a simple phrase like "expectant anticipation." On the page opposite the image, reflect upon what God is revealing to you through this process. It may be something you were not aware of, or it may be an affirmation of what you already know. Even though you are transitioning your prayer process from drawing to writing, continue to ask God to be a part of it, revealing to you what you need to know. Sometimes the words come quickly, and I dialogue with God, the image, and what the day holds for me. Other times it is harder to begin, or I may want to look deeper at what God is telling me.

If it is difficult for you to find a place to begin, consider these basic questions that will help in the dialogue process:

1. What is your initial impression of what you have drawn? What is your emotional reaction to the image, your mental acceptance of what you see, your physical response? Write down in simple, one-word statements your response: uneasy, hopeful, agitated, uncertain, joyful, light-hearted, tired, energetic. Expand on this if desired.
2. Look at the colors you have used. Take each color individually and reflect on what the color symbolizes for you. For example, the color blue may bring up an immediate response of peacefulness, connection with nature, water, calm; or it may bring an immediate response of sadness or depression. Note your personal associations for the colors you used.

   If it is a color you don't like, or wouldn't normally use, or found yourself not wanting to use but used it anyway, reflect on that and why God urged you to use that particular color. For example, orange is a color that feels nervous to me, and I don't usually have good associations with it. My first response to seeing that color is to determine if that is the feeling the color is expressing. I do this by looking at how I've used orange and what other colors are around it. If the sense of nervousness or agitation intuitively feels correct, I reflect on that. Sometimes I know instinctively that this is not the correct interpretation and I find that, on deeper reflection, what is being communicated is positive energy or power.

   Ask yourself how the colors go together—do they seem to fit into a harmony, or do they feel disconnected and chaotic? What does this tell you about how you're feeling? You can refer to the color symbolism chart in the appendix for deeper reflection and insight, but remember always to rely first on your own personal symbolic associations.
3. Is there anything in your prayer image that makes you feel uneasy? Does it bring up an event or situation in your life that you do not want to deal with right now, or one that you are trying to avoid? Consider why you feel this way.

4. How does this image relate to your prayer focus?
5. Most importantly, what do you think God is trying to make you aware of through the image? Will knowing what and how you feel about this issue or concern help you deal with it? Dialogue with God and the image before you.

The hardest part of the visual imaging process is beginning. As with any new prayer discipline, it takes time, practice, and a continued effort before it becomes comfortable or natural. Try this basic exercise for several days: You can change your prayer focus to something very specific if you have something special going on, or you can ask God to reveal what God wants you to be aware of. Either way, don't get discouraged, even if it feels awkward for a time or if you feel that you are not getting much out of it. You will find that the process gets easier and more comfortable, and you will also discover that your heart's landscape has its own language—one that is both unique to you and also deeply connected with archetypal images common to all human beings. Part of my heart's language is the image of the egg, which appears regularly and always holds out the hope of possibilities, things to come, things waiting to be birthed. Learning your heart's language is part of the journey, and with time you will understand and recognize it with clarity and ease.

JOURNAL EXCERPT: ANNA'S PRAYER ASKING GOD, "HELP ME UNDERSTAND MY FEELINGS TODAY."

Fig. 8. Anna's expressive prayer.

"This drawing makes me sad. The colors are sad too. Light blue rain/tear drops. The gray is depressing. The only bright spot is the sun. Besides being so depressing, I wonder why the sun is under the water. But the image feels right for some reason. I think it is about what is going on with Bill. He's dying. He has always been my favorite uncle, close. No matter where I am or what I do, I always feel sadness. Thinking about this and looking at the picture, I think maybe the sun is him. He has always been the bright light of the family. Maybe it is me. Can I still function in the midst of sadness? Perhaps the sun is God. If so, I feel hopeful. God, help me hold on to the light of the sun."

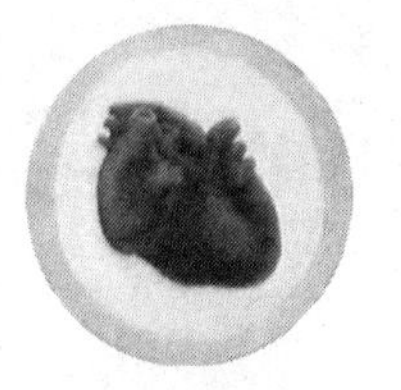

5

— ROUGH AND UNEVEN ROADS —
Doubts and Longings

Although it's my morning to sleep in, I'm awake at 6:00 with my coffee, prayer book, journal, and pastels outside on the back patio. What a beautiful morning—it's early spring, trees are beginning to bud, the massive rose bush, full of yellow roses, is sending long, exploring tendrils way up into the top of the trees. A bird is singing at the top of its lungs, and I finally spot him—a big fat mockingbird sitting in the very top of the tree with the roses. I smile at him as he sings loud enough to drown out the sound of passing cars—no easy feat.

As I listen to the bird song, rain begins to fall—a light cool spring rain, not hard enough to drive me indoors, but wonderful and fresh. The trumpet vine covering the lattice next to me is literally a solid wall of orange flowers, absolutely amazing to see. I know the hummingbirds will soon be back from their wintering in Mexico and will love the feast. I am content, surrounded by signs of spring

I open my journal to a blank page, spread my oil pastels out in front of me, and sit back, allowing myself to just "be." I sit with eyes closed, and ask for the awareness of God's presence. I have no special focus in my prayer time this morning, so I ask God to present whatever it is I need this day.

When I'm ready, I open my eyes and pick up the orange crayon. I hate orange. It makes me nervous. Resigning myself to the process, even with orange, I close my eyes again and allow the crayon to meander directionless over the page. When I open my eyes, I have a hard time finding anything in the scribble I've drawn, so I turn the page, this way and that, again and again until I am holding the journal upside down. It is then that I see her—or me. I pick up the red and begin to draw her in. She is curled up in a fetal position, very oval and womblike. I see a heart in her chest very clearly and, much to my dismay, I pick up the orange crayon and color in the heart, wondering why God is making me use this color. I'm not surprised to see my recurring egg shape in the lower part of the woman—in her womb—and I pick up the purple and fill in the egg. I fill in the woman with more red and then I am urged to add yellow to the heart. With great energy I finish by outlining the woman with a solid mandala of yellow rays.

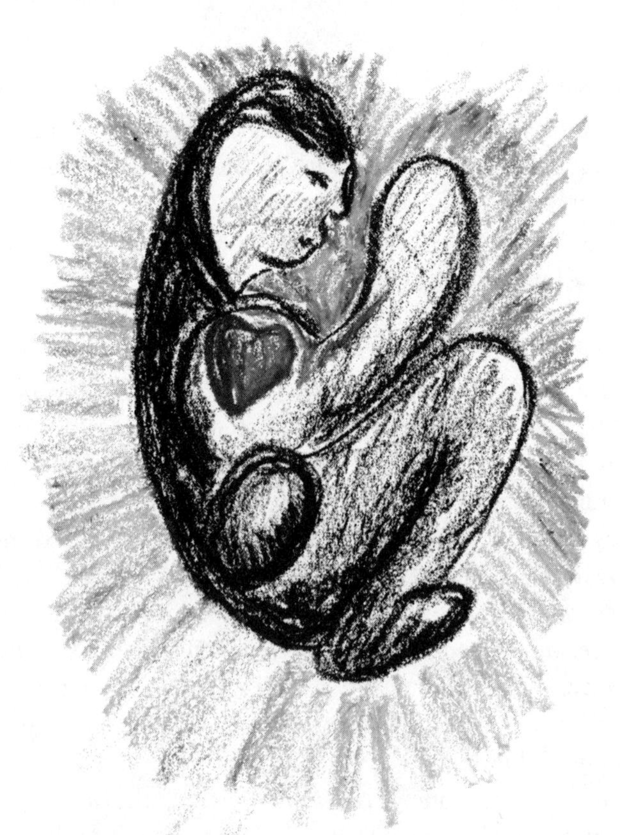

Fig. 9. Early morning prayer.

What am I to think of her? What is God telling me? It doesn't seem like anything new, as I recognize her from images I've drawn before. I'm very aware that I'm in a period of transition, and that I can't sleep at night when I'm assailed by doubts; I long to find my call again and uncover the new possibilities my situation offers me. I look at the egg and immediately relate the purple to Lenten penitence, but it doesn't feel right. It is a rich color, and as I talk with God about what it might mean, I know that the egg contains all the unknowns that I am holding within me, things that are not yet ready to be birthed, but will be soon. The heart—that *orange* heart—is full of life and energy and hope; there is a pulsing vitality there in spite of my self-doubt and fears. On this morning, when so many choices lie before me, God is reassuring my self-worth, my future, calling me to be patient in my waiting, to live with my doubts and longings, and to trust as my Creator shapes something new within me.

It's difficult to trust God in the midst of transition, chaos, doubt or despair, or when we feel that we've lost control over our lives. In these times we lose our sense of direction, seemingly traveling down a rough road full of rocks, ruts, detours, and dead ends. All the doubts and longings deep within our hearts begin to surface: doubts about our selves, our lives, our self-worth. We long to know the answers, to regain control over our lives.

Control is such an overpowering need of ours. We like and want to have at least a little bit of control over our lives, our work, and our loved ones. Even though we know in our heads that God should be in control, our hearts don't always agree. We want a say in how things turn out, whether our concerns are genuine or selfish.

When we doubt ourselves, when the longings of our heart leave us restless and feeling lost, we respond by trying to exert control. I have a quirky way of trying to control my life when things get out of hand that has become a joke between my husband, Allan, and me. When we first moved to our town, I didn't know anyone and I didn't have a job to go to. It was Christmas and I faced a house full of boxes and a deadline with our five daughters coming to town. I was feeling quite unsure of myself, and very unsettled. Complicating matters, two of our daughters didn't leave after Christmas; instead, they unexpectedly moved in with us, adding to the chaos.

Allan and I have a deal worked out where I cook and he cleans up after the meal. It usually works great, but during this chaotic transitional time, I began to "help" him load the dishwasher. After he would finish loading the dishes at random, I would rearrange everything into a logical order. He questioned me about this, arguing that the dishes would get clean anyway, and I answered that I liked them better this way. But his questioning persisted, and after a while I got tired of it and firmly said, "I have absolutely no control over anything in my life right now—at least give me the dishwasher!"

We know in our heads that we should give our self-doubts and need for control to God. Jesus tells us not to let our hearts be troubled or worry about our lives: "[Y]our heavenly Father knows that you need all these things. But strive first for the kingdom of God and his righteousness, and all these things will be given to you as well. So do not worry about tomorrow, for tomorrow will bring worries of its own" (Matthew 6:32b–34a). Fretting doesn't do anyone any good. But our hearts are a little harder to convince sometimes.

NAVIGATING THE ROUGH AND UNEVEN ROADS OF OUR HEART

Exercise Two—Scribble Prayer

The roads and precipices within our hearts are hard to navigate, and our senses of direction and purpose are easily thrown off. We find it hard to know which way to go. How often do we find ourselves at a crossroads; a crossroads of self, life circumstances, of our relationship with God? Our sense of personal power, of direction, of the ability to navigate the rough roads of life, comes with a deeper knowledge of who we are and what we value, along with a conviction of our intrinsic worth. This sense of self may take years to develop, but when it is in place, it changes us. And so, we turn in prayer to God for direction.

Preparing and Focusing the heART

Take your journal and turn to the first blank double page. Select and prepare your drawing materials. Now consider your prayer focus. For this prayer, think of something in your life that is causing you to doubt yourself or God, causing you to feel uneasy, or making you feel as if you have no control. For instance, you may be experiencing some changes at work that are causing you concern, so your prayer focus may be: "God, give me the resources to cope with this new program better." After writing the date and your prayer focus at the top of the blank page on the right side of your journal, set the journal down and sit back quietly.

Close your eyes and take deep, even breaths. As you have previously done, focus yourself first on the outer world, notice things around you and on your mind, then let them go. Allow yourself to draw deeper within, taking note of how you are feeling, both physically and mentally. Finally, as you continue taking deep breaths, draw your focus even deeper, toward God. Hold up your prayer focus and ask God to open your heart to a greater awareness of God's presence. Sit in God's presence in this way until you feel that you are ready to "listen" to God through the image.

Prayer of the heART

Open your eyes and pick up whatever color jumps out at you, whatever color your eye is drawn to, even if you don't like it or wouldn't normally use that color. Remember you are allowing God to draw the image *through* you, so you shouldn't try to control the choice of colors or images that appear. Place your hand on the page, allow yourself to feel its boundaries, and close your eyes, allowing your crayon to meander or "scribble" over the page. Continue until you feel finished, then open your eyes and put down your drawing material.

At this point, look for an image in the scribble, in the same way you would find images in the clouds. You may have to look at your drawing from different angles until you see something. When an image appears, mark a small "t" at the top of the page even though it may not be the angle from which you originally drew the scribble. This will be the angle from which you will work from this point on.

Now, pick up another color and again let God direct you to complete the image that you see. Add whatever details God leads you to add—colors, lines, shapes, images—in order to bring the image to life. You do not have to stay within the scribble lines once you have begun to pray the image. Let the Spirit guide you to work on the image in this way, adding whatever is necessary, and ignoring whatever scribble lines do not fit, until it feels finished.

Listening to the Image

Give thanks to God for the gift of this image. As before, write down your first impressions or feelings the image provokes in you. On the page opposite the image, begin your dialogue with God and the image. If you find it hard to know where to begin your dialogue, consider these questions:

1. What is your initial impression of what you have drawn? What is your emotional reaction to the image, your mental acceptance of what you see, your physical response?
2. How would you describe the colors you have used? Take each color individually and reflect upon what the color symbolizes for you. What are your personal associations to the colors you used? If you see a color you don't like, wouldn't normally use, or found yourself not wanting to use but used it anyway, reflect upon why God urged you to use that particular color. Ask yourself how the colors go together—do they seem to fit into a harmony, or do they feel disconnected and chaotic? What does this tell you about how you are feeling? You can refer to the color symbolism chart in the appendix for deeper reflection and insight, but remember always to rely on your own personal symbolic associations first.
3. Can you relate your feelings brought up by the prayer image to something particular in your life, especially as it pertains to your prayer focus?
4. What do you think God is trying to make you aware of through the image?

Continue to dialogue with God and the image before you. If your dialogue raises more questions or issues, use them as your next prayer focus.

JOURNAL EXCERPT: "GOD, I DON'T KNOW WHAT I AM SUPPOSED TO DO NOW THAT I DON'T HAVE A REGULAR JOB. HELP."

Fig. 10. Kelly's scribble prayer.

"What is this all about? Flames? A bud about to open? A mother and child? Seeds? The flames encompass the female figures, reds, yellow, oranges. Fire is destructive, but this doesn't feel that way. It feels right, purifying. The bud is small, off to the side, but bright green and full of life. The mother and child are outlined with blue, which is calming and nurturing, reassuring. The seeds are red. Seeds are full of possibility. Red is life-giving, like blood. Perhaps there is hope that I am on the right road. I'll see where this leads me."

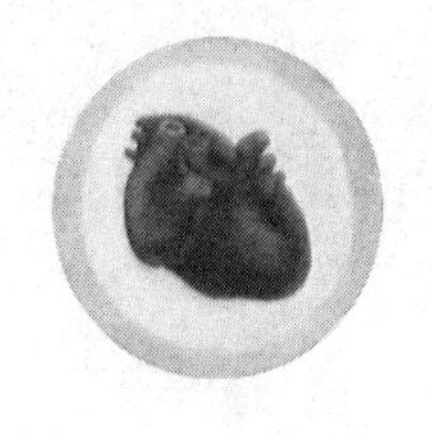

6

— GOD AND THE ANGELS —

God in the Ordinary

It was Friday night, and Sara had gone out with friends and was planning on staying over at their house. Emily, although she had offers, decided to stay home—unusual for a teenager. I planned to work that evening on some reading and a paper for one of my seminary classes, but Emily had other ideas for me. She came into my room, sat down on the floor, and asked me if we could do something that night—like watch a movie. I debated on what to do. The rational thing would be to get my work done, but I could be irrational and take the evening off. I chose what I then thought was the irrational decision.

One of the things Emily and I have always liked to do together is watch old movies and musicals, and one of our favorites is *The Man of La Mancha*. We picked it up and then stopped by the grocery store for two gallon-size cartons of ice cream, cookie dough and mint chocolate chip. Once we got home, we prepared for our big evening. We set up our little love seat in front of the TV, got the movie ready, and bundled ourselves in blankets. It was very, very cold that evening, and our house didn't have heat in the front room, so blankets were especially necessary since we would be eating ice cream. Once all was set, we settled ourselves on the little sofa, propped the ice cream cartons—no bowls of course—in our laps and began our movie.

Eating and singing along at the top of our voices, "I am Don Quixote, the man of La Mancha . . ."

After eating as much ice cream as we could, we lay down next to each other, my arm around her, and watched the rest of the movie—scrunched together on the tiny love seat, wrapped tight with the blankets, like two worms in a cocoon. We sang all of the songs. We laughed. We cried.

And I laid there and looked at my beautiful daughter. Smiling, singing, content to be lying next to me—so full of life, of potential, of love, of God. All of the problems of growing up, all the stress of school and finances and life were—for that moment—gone. And I knew that we were surrounded by and filled with God's presence, by God's grace, by God's love. I was blessed that grace-filled, totally unexpected evening, one that I would have missed had I worked instead. It was a sacramental moment, and fortunately I was alert and aware enough to recognize God's presence with us. It is an evening Emily and I still remember.

I have learned a lot since then about what the Buddhists call mindfulness and what Brother Lawrence calls the practice of the presence of God. God, in whom we live and move and have our being, became flesh in the man Jesus of Nazareth. In the Gospel of John we read that "All things came into being through him, and without him not one thing came into being" (John 1:3). As we take this to heart, we can acknowledge and be aware of the presence of God in all aspects of our lives. Once awakened, once aware of this truth, we can see the concrete presence of grace, of God in our world.

In the Celtic tradition, it is believed that all creation is inherently good because it comes from a good and loving God. And if creation comes from God, all that is created may be a means of revelation, all things have the potential of being sacramental. All that we do, all aspects of work and play, life and death, all the events of our lives can reveal Christ's presence and offer us a greater understanding and experience of God and ourselves.

In the Benedictine tradition there is a focus on incarnation, God in everything—all we see and touch and taste and do. Benedictines seek to see Christ in each person and strive to follow Christ in all things. We are also called to practice awareness of God's constant presence within and among us, whether we are washing dishes, folding clothes, driving our kids to school, mopping the floor, performing heart surgery, chairing an executive board meeting, or making the closing argument in court.

Brother Lawrence, a Benedictine monk, wrote a little treasure of a book called *The Practice of the Presence of God* in which he urges, "Please remember what I recommended to you, which is to think often about God in the daytime, at night, in all your occupations, in your exercises, and even during your times of amusement. He is always near you and with you."[1] Living an incarnational life is living with a heart always open to God.

I was driving to Amarillo one day, all alone on the long and boring drive. Outside of Lubbock, as the sun began to set, the sky came alive with the most incredible sunset I have ever seen. It began slowly, reds and oranges spreading across the horizon, silhouetting the hills in a deep, dark purple. Then it grew, spreading all around the horizon, not just in the west. The colors glowed and changed—reds, pinks, oranges, and purples, constantly changing and moving to an unheard song. It was so incredible that I had to pull over and stop the car. I got out and stood there, turning around and around, soaking in and being soaked by the colors. Slowly, it began to fade, and for a long time I couldn't move.

I can describe the sunset, the sky, the colors, and the hill silhouettes. I can explain in scientific terms how the atmosphere, the moisture, dust, and heat all combined that day to create what I saw, but I know there was more. There was God—there was glory, radiance, passion, there was expansive, all-encompassing light and color. There was infinity, grace, and eternity. All of it settled in my heart, surrounded and encompassed me, assuring me of God's love and presence within and around me.

---

1. Brother Lawrence, *The Practice of the Presence of God* (Orleans, Mass: Paraclete Press, 1993), 104.

We're all so busy, so preoccupied with the things we have to do, places we have to go. It's so easy to close the eyes of our heart to the world and people around us. Paul urges us to live mindfully of the presence of God: "For what can be known about God is plain to them, because God has shown it to them. Ever since the creation of the world his eternal power and divine nature, invisible though they are, have been understood and seen and seen through the things he has made." (Romans 1:19–20).

To live mindful lives we need to change our attitude, our vision, hearing, and speaking in such a way that we open ourselves to an awareness of God in all that we encounter. Everything can speak of God, of God's beauty, goodness, and mystery. A movie and a carton of ice cream is more than just watching and eating. A sunset is more than just the setting sun. Human beings are more than just human beings. To quote Brother Lawrence again, "If we do not know that, we must learn it."[2]

Keeping our hearts open to the ordinary things of this life and the potential they have of revealing God allows us to live a life focused on God. By intentionally becoming more mindful to the presence of God in and through all things, we not only come to know God more intimately, but we come to know our true selves in a deeper way—a way that is connected by the thread of the incarnation running through all of creation.

Experiencing God's Presence in the Ordinary

Exercise Three—Praying the Mandala

Preparing and Focusing the heART

Turn your journal to the first blank double page. Decide whether you will use regular crayons or oil pastels and lay them out on the table before you. Depending on the size of your journal page, have either a 10–12" paper plate or a small paper plate available to use as a guide for drawing a circle on the page. Now consider your prayer focus. For this prayer, ask God to help you realize his presence in your life—in the ordinary tasks and events of your day.

---

2. Ibid, 105.

At the top of the blank page on the right side of your journal, write the date and your prayer focus. Set your journal down and sit back quietly.

Close your eyes and take deep even breaths. Begin your progression by focusing on the outward world and all that it entails, then draw inward to concentrate on yourself and how you are, and finally focus on God. Ask for an awareness of God's presence within and around you. Hold up your prayer focus, keeping your mind free from trying to formulate words; center on God and hold the focus in your mind. Continue to keep your eyes closed, breathing deeply and evenly until you feel ready.

Prayer of the heART

Open your eyes and pick up whatever color your eye is drawn to. Remember that God is in control—choose the color God leads you to choose. Trace the paper plate on your journal page, then fill in the circle with colors, lines, and forms. You may begin anywhere, in the center or around the edges or at one side. Go outside the circle if need be. You may feel led to draw recognizable images such as flowers, trees, the sun, and so on. You may find that you are only drawing abstract, seemingly random shapes and forms. Either way is okay—just remember to follow the nudging of the Spirit, allowing God to guide you. Continue this process until you're finished. Look at the drawing from all angles until you find the angle that feels right and mark the top with a small "t." It may not be the angle from which you drew the image, but you will look at it from this angle when dialoguing with it.

Listening to the Image

Thank God for the gift of this image. Under your written prayer focus, write down your first impression of the feeling or idea expressed by what you have drawn. On the page opposite the image you have drawn, reflect on what God is revealing to you through your image. Consider these questions:

1. What is your initial impression and emotional reaction to the image?

2. What personal and universal symbolism do the colors hold? What does this symbolism reveal to you about yourself, your experience of God, or God's desires for you?
3. What have you learned about the presence of God in your daily life?
4. What do you think God wants you to take from this prayer time? Is it something you can apply to your life?

After reflecting on the questions above, continue to dialogue with God and the image before you. If your dialogue raises more questions or issues, use these as your next prayer focus.

JOURNAL EXCERPT: BRIGID'S EXPERIENCE OF GOD IN AN ORDINARY MOMENT

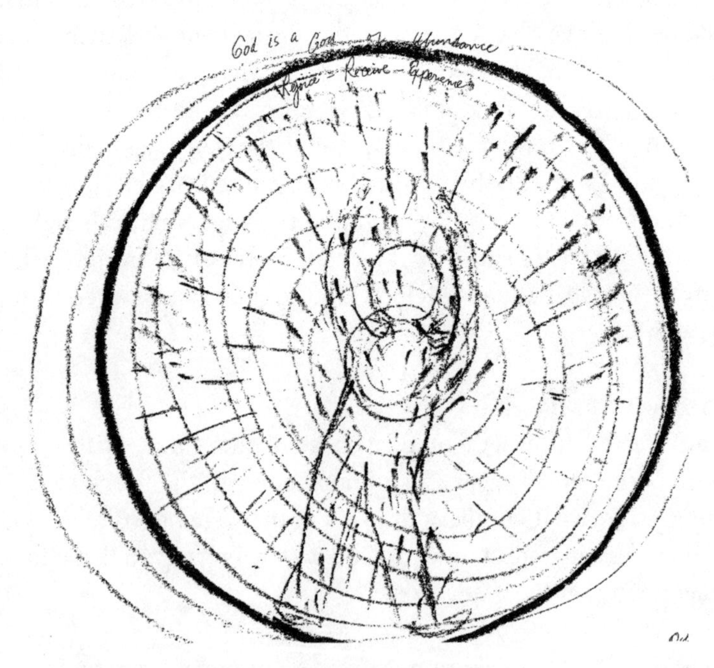

Fig. 11. Brigid's mandala prayer.

"My mandala was preordained to be a representation of the experience I had—an 'ordinary' experience that caused me to think of God's presence. I was taking a shower and feeling the lovely, hot, abundant water cascade over my body—refreshing me, caressing me, anointing me, cleansing me. And I thought that the water, in its abundance and intimacy, was a great symbol—and even experience—of the presence of God.

I often don't take enough time in the shower to let such awareness register. But when it does, I could cry for joy and gratitude.

I used blue—because I was showing the water—I chose purple for myself. I'm not sure why, but when I read the symbolism I liked that it mentions 'abundance of purple' in spring flowers—and even more that it symbolized the energy of red and the severity of blue—'mystic union.' I also resonate with 'restless motive energy of something seeking to become free at a new level of being.'

That is my prayer—to become free at a new level of being.

My journey of life has provided me with both experiences and learnings that have bound and imprisoned my soul, my spirit—and with experiences, learnings, healings, that have called me to freedom and growth. I believe there are levels of healing and freedom that still await me. I want to be open."

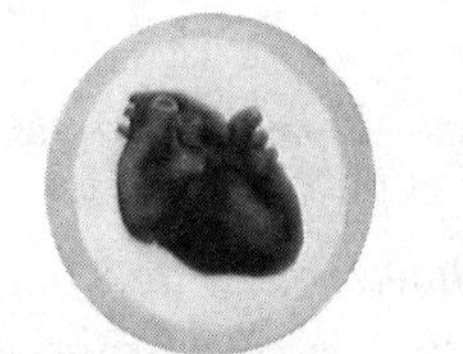

7

— DRAGONS, LIONS, POISONOUS BEASTS —

Forgiving and Letting Go

When I was little, I loved to play make believe, and one of my favorite places to play was at the house down the street from mine with Hazel and Deena. Their house was tiny and unpainted, always looking a bit sad, but since there was no grass in the yard, it was the perfect place to make mud pies. We would set up our kitchen—made from old boxes, crates, and barrels—behind the house, and we collected old broken bowls and cups, old tin cans, and spoons and sticks for our utensils. To the side of our kitchen we dug a pit that we filled with water and dirt until our mud was just the right consistency. If you've ever made mud pies, you know that you must get the mud just right—not too thick or clumpy, but not too runny.

We'd make a variety of mud pies: some would be plain mud, nothing added; after all, some people like things simple. To others we'd add carefully selected rocks, sticks, leaves, and, when we were lucky enough to find them, dried-up pill bugs—they added wonderful texture. When we had filled the bowls, we'd carefully clean off as much of the mud from the outside as possible and line up the pies for the finishing touches—we had to add these if we wanted anyone to admire our pies or take them seriously. So we would walk through the fields and around the neighborhood and gather whatever flowers we could find to decorate our pies. We selected the flowers carefully, and even more carefully placed them in lovely patterns on top of the mud.

Then we'd display our finished pies out by the street to our mothers and neighbors, always hoping that someone would be deceived by their appetizing appearance and buy one.

I can still see them lined up on the curb, enticing, fascinating, and wonderful to look at. My favorites were always the ones with pomegranate flowers on top with their bright red-orange blossoms screaming "Look at me! I'm beautiful! I'm tasty! I am what you want! Buy me!" We didn't sell many mud pies—after all, underneath the beautiful flowers they were still only mud and leaves, sticks and pill bugs, of value only to our imaginations.

In Matthew's gospel, we read about the time Jesus dines with a Pharisee, after he has just healed the sick and cast out demons. The Pharisee reprimands him because he does not wash his hands before the meal. But Jesus turns the reprimand back on the Pharisee saying: "For you clean the outside of the cup and of the plate, but inside they are full of greed and self-indulgence. You blind Pharisee! First clean the inside of the cup, so that the outside also may become clean" (Matthew 23:25–26). The Pharisee doesn't understand that what comes from inside, from the heart, is what matters.

Jesus turns the image of the cup, the bowl, into a metaphor for us. For years I made pottery, and I find that throwing a vessel on a potter's wheel corresponds very closely to what Jesus is saying. I'd make the inside of the vessel first, and the outside would take its form from the shaping and molding of the inside. I'd place a ball of clay in the middle of the wheel and, as the wheel spun, I centered and secured the clay. Then, with my hands gently cupping the clay between them, I'd press my thumbs slowly but firmly into the center of top of the clay creating an opening, an inside. By gently expanding the opening outward and extending the sides of the vessel, working from the inside out, I lifted and shaped the clay. You can't use too much pressure on the clay or too little. You can't spin the wheel too fast or too slow. You cannot use too much water or too little. It's a delicate balance of knowledge and intuition. When making a vessel, the inside is made first, and the outside takes its form from the shaping and molding of the inside. It is only when the inside has been formed, that the outside can be refined.

After completing the vessel, I would decorate and glaze it. Although the outward appearance is displayed for others, the inside is what gives it its value, its purpose. The inside offers itself for use and gives the outside its worth no matter how lovely or unattractive it is.

We are God's vessels. Our outside is the part of us we present to the world and to each other; our inside is our hearts, where we think and understand, where our desires and passions originate, where our self-awareness comes from. Our inside informs our outside.

Just as the inside of the cup gives the cup its purpose, our inside, our heart gives us our true value. And just as the cup is empty and waiting to be filled, so are our hearts. But what are we filling our hearts with?

Sometimes we tend to fill our hearts with anger, hurt, sadness, resentment, guilt, or "dragons, lions and poisonous beasts, all the treasures of evil" as Macarius says. We hold these things tightly rather than letting them go. Jesus says, "forgive from your heart," and "forgive seventy times seven," but it is hard to do. Our outward appearance is deceiving; no one looking at us would suspect that we are holding in such turmoil. Our outside rarely reflects the inner state of our hearts when it comes to forgiveness.

I've been told that if you haven't forgotten, you haven't forgiven, but I don't believe this is true. Forgiveness is not a magic formula that erases the past. It's a process that can, depending on the offense, take years. The process of forgiving is like cleaning out the inside of the bowl, the inside of our hearts. Barbara Cawthorne Crafton explains forgiveness like this:

To forgive is not to forget
        is not a feeling
        is not a job
To forgive is a gift

To forgive is not an acquittal
        is not "getting out of consequences"

is not about the perpetrator
is not about the severity of the offense
To forgive is a theological decision—a choice
based on God's will

To forgive is not a moment
is not the restoration of presence
(things like they were)
is not about the past
Forgiveness is a process.[1]

We can present ourselves to the world as being whole and healthy and living with integrity, but if we forego the hard process of forgiveness, we risk having no more substance than the mud pies made appealing with the bright red-orange blossoms of pomegranate flowers. Without forgiveness, our hearts cannot be fully our own.

Cleaning out the Dragons and Poisonous Beasts

Exercise Four—Forgiveness

Cleaning is neither something I like to do nor do very well, whether I'm cleaning my house or cleaning out my heart. I also tend to procrastinate because it's such a difficult task for me.

For many, this visual prayer exercise will be one of the most difficult you will attempt, because some hurts you'll encounter are very deep and very old. You may even need to forgive yourself, or, worse, even God.

Because this process of prayer may bring up painful memories, you may want to start with a small, simple incident before undertaking a more thorough "spiritual spring cleaning." I suggest seeing your spiritual director, priest, or a psychologist if your prayers trigger something very deep—don't try to walk through it completely on your own. Also remember that one drawing may not be enough for the process of forgiveness. It may take several, and it may even take years. Let some time pass between each prayer, reflect on the

1. Barbara Cawthorne Crafton, Diocese of West Texas Clergy Retreat, Camp Capers, Waring, TX, March 8, 2004.

previous prayer images, and dialogue with God until you feel ready to go to the next step. You may use any of the visual prayer techniques at any time.

Preparing and Focusing the heART

Organize your art materials. During the centering time, sit prayerfully and ask God to reveal to you someone or something that you need to forgive. Focus on one person or one incident to hold up to God. Imagine this person in God's presence, being lovingly held in God's hands. Sit with this image and allow yourself to feel whatever it is God reveals to you. You may be very surprised at what you're shown.

When prayerfully imaging a particularly painful incident, I found that I couldn't see the person in God's hands, but only relive the pain of the relationship. This is okay. Remember, part of the process of forgiveness may involve getting out all the feelings of hurt and anger before being able to let go.

Prayer of the heART

When you're ready, begin to draw what you see or feel using any of the visual prayer techniques you choose. Continue praying your image on paper until it feels complete, remembering that this particular focus may take several drawings to fully explore.

Listening to the Image

When dialoguing with your prayer image, consider the following questions.

1. What did you draw? Describe it as a story if you can. This allows you to reflect on the experience and see what stands out as being important.
2. How did you feel as you drew it? How do you feel now? If the feeling is different, why and how?
3. Do the colors, shapes, and images tell you anything significant about yourself, the person, or the situation?
4. Having prayed this image, are you any closer to being able to forgive this person? Is the situation any clearer?

5. If you are still not ready to let go and forgive, what reasons do you have that are holding you back? Throughout the next few weeks or months continue the process by praying ongoing images. Reflect on the images and any progress you may make.

When (or if) you reach a point of forgiveness, use the same prayerful process to forgive this person and let go of the situation by offering them back to God. Reflect on how you feel.

JOURNAL EXCERPT: FORGIVENESS SERIES

Fig. 12. Forgiveness prayer 1.

"I tried to hold him up to God. But I couldn't. All I felt was anger. Anger at how I was treated. Anger at myself for letting it happen. He was always trying to overpower me, push me down, keep me quiet. I know I didn't help. I fought it. I fought him. But this is how I feel. He is a monster. Dark green, jealousy, venom—maybe, it feels right. Ugly, with long, sharp red teeth. I am cowering in the corner, my back against a red wall. Deep purple surrounds me. Cruelty seems right. I am light blue with orange around me. I hate orange. It is agitating. But it fits. There is a little bit of pink between me and the wall. It is the feminine or stress. Pink can mean physical illness and stress and

I was sick from all the turmoil at the time. This is an ugly and disturbing image, but it is how I feel. I will keep trying. I know that I need to forgive him before I can get on with my life."

Fig. 13. Forgiveness prayer 2.

"Again, I tried to hold him up to God. Again, it didn't work. But this time there was a difference. The image is clear. He and I are bound together as long as I don't forgive. He is still that same dark, ugly green, but this time he is a worm, cocoonlike. I too am cocoonlike and still light blue and pink. Our experience has bound us together. This part of my life has shaped who I am now. But I don't have to let it keep me bound. I can break away."

"It's been some time since I tried to forgive him. I put it aside for a while. Today my prayer focus was open-ended, "What do you have to tell me today, God?" It wasn't about forgiveness. But here it is. "Bruised and Wounded," I call it. The hurt, the anger is still there and unexpectedly resurfaces to pierce my spirit. It does. Out of nowhere the painful memories surface to disrupt my days. I need to let go so that I can be free like the bird. I drew the scribbles in black. I knew then that the image would be serious. The bird is flying; she is yellow and orange, bright and full of energy. I like her. She is me. But there is an arrow, black, dark blue, and red. It is my anger. At first it

Fig. 14. Forgiveness prayer 3.

Fig. 15. Forgiveness prayer 4.

seemed that it was going to pierce the bird. But as Carol pointed out, the arrow has not penetrated. It has hurt but has not killed. There is hope. I feel that this is a big step."

"I asked God again today to help me forgive. I felt so sad. He is so sad. So lonely and insecure. I no longer see him as a monster. This image is so right. He is still the dark green ugly monster, but he is melted—about all that is left is his eye which

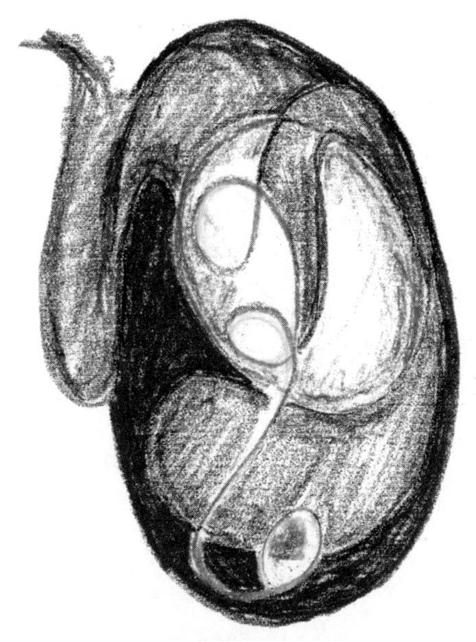

Fig. 16. Forgiveness prayer 5.

is enclosed in a dark green tear. I am crying. Big red tears. It is painful, but healing."

"Today, finally, I have let go. The red egg is here again. It is always a good symbol for me. A symbol of new growth and new beginnings. Inside I am curled up like an embryo waiting for birth. Now it is I who am green—not the venomous ugly green that he was, but a deep rich green. There is an orange and yellow seed pod entwined around me. And another egg. An egg within an egg. Pink, new, feminine, full of innocence. I feel free from him at last. I can let go and forgive. Another thought—could this be him and not me? Can I allow this to be him, held up to God as a new child ready to begin again? Surrounded by God's protective shell? Yes. I think so."

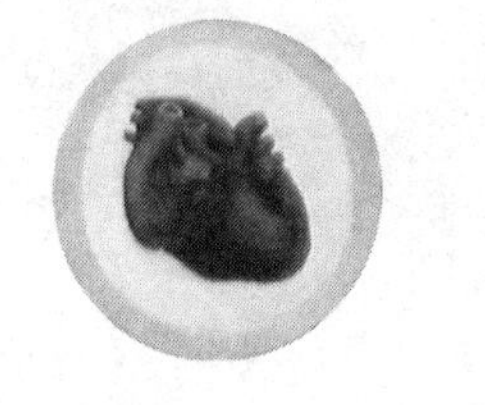

8

— ALL THE TREASURES OF EVIL —

Fear

My father used to take us sailing in his large sailboat on Canyon Lake. I was a reluctant sailor, afraid of deep water, but I would go because my girls loved it. And there were times that I enjoyed it as well—when the winds were calm and the sailing was smooth—but I would hold on with white knuckles and a knot in my stomach if the wind and water ever got rough. I remember one day in particular when we went out early one afternoon and stayed on the water for hours. As the day grew later and we started to head back to the marina, it got dark and a storm blew in unexpectedly. The wind blew and the water churned. The boat was sailing on its side and the sails were flapping back and forth as the wind whipped them. I got very frightened. My father and uncle struggled to keep the boat under control as the storm got worse, and I could see the concern in their faces. I sat paralyzed with fear as the white-capped waves tossed the boat.

Just as the thunderstom paralyzed me that day on the lake, many of us find ourselves paralyzed with fear when the storms of life batter us and the waves threaten to overwhelm us. But Jesus, who calmed the storm and walked on water, said, "Take heart, it is I; do not be afraid" (Matthew 14:27).

Fear isn't something we like to experience, or deal with, or talk about. But fear is a part of our lives whether we like it or not.

❧

It was so late, and I was so tired. Sleep was like an elusive butterfly, fluttering closely around my head, but just out of reach. I had spent the day at the hospital admitting Sara for depression and suicidal thoughts. As I began to doze off a little, Emily came into my room and stood by my bed. "Mom," she said quietly, "I swallowed a bottle of aspirin. I want to go to the hospital." My heart froze, and my stomach lurched in fear.

In my last year of seminary, I faced what I believe has been the greatest challenge of my life so far. My two daughters, then sixteen and eighteen, were dealing with issues of childhood abuse. In spite of several years of counseling, they still weren't able to deal with it and turned, both at the same time, to other ways of trying to forget. They used alcohol, marijuana, cocaine, cut themselves, and attempted suicide. I was trying to keep up with my classes, driving three days a week to San Antonio for one daughter, attending two therapy sessions a week for my other daughter, doing field work, and on and on. During this time, as I was talking with a man who was trying to guide me through this, he said to me, "Kelly, you're tough as steel."

Tough as steel. What a joke, I thought. I felt like I was going to fall apart any minute. I was terrified of losing my daughters. I was hanging on by a thread, trying to keep myself together so that I could do whatever I could to protect them and keep them alive. It was not toughness, it was fear—fear of losing what I loved. I kept going, persisting, because I was in a survival mode—like a mother hen gathers her chicks or a lioness protects her cubs.

Tough as steel. My fear was legitimate. I was consumed by guilt, even though I really had no control over the situation. But I had to face it.

Fear can paralyze. Fear itself is not the problem, but what we do with our fear or what we let our fear do to us can overwhelmingly affect our lives. In her cancer journal, Audre Lorde writes, "Maybe this is the chance to live and speak those things I really do believe, that power comes from moving into whatever I fear most that cannot be avoided."[1]

For me, moving into my fear meant letting go of my need to find an immediate answer. It meant placing myself and my girls in God's hands, and allowing myself to trust in God's unconditional love for us and for our well being. In this process, a transition slowly took place—a transition from fear that paralyzes to one that, while still a reality, no longer had ultimate control of me. I came to understand the meaning of courage.

Courage is a state of the heart, one which gives the spirit the ability to face difficult situations with confidence. Confidence, no matter what the outcome, in God's ultimate desire for good. Courage and strength come from knowing that we are loved and beloved by God. Jesus said, "Do not fear those who kill the body but cannot kill the soul. . . . Are not two sparrows sold for a penny? Yet not one of them will fall to the ground unperceived by your Father. And even the hairs of your head are all counted. So do not be afraid; you are of more value than many sparrows" (Matthew 10:28a, 29–31).

That time in my life has past. My girls are now healthy and happy. But I still remember, it was the promise of God's love, both for me, and especially for my girls, that allowed me to face my fears and have the strength and courage to get up and get through each day.

We also fear our own selves, our own inadequacies. This fear is insidious, but it isn't obvious. How many times have you doubted yourself? How many times have you stopped yourself from doing or saying something because you felt like you wouldn't be taken seriously, or felt unsure or somehow lacking? Although fear can paralyze us, we can use it as an impetus to change and to discover and accept ourselves as we are made in the image of God.

---

1. Audre Lorde, "The Cancer Journals (excerpt)," in *Cries of the Spirit: A Celebration of Women's Spirituality*, ed. Marilyn Sewell (Boston: Beacon Press, 1991), 123.

In Isaiah, God says, "Do not fear, for I have redeemed you; I have called you by name, you are mine. When you pass through the waters, I will be with you; and through the rivers, they shall not overwhelm you; when you walk through fire you shall not be burned, and the flame shall not consume you. . . . [Y]ou are precious in my sight, and honored, and I love you" (Isaiah 43:1b–2, 4a). Do you believe this? Can you accept the fact that God loves you, that you are precious and honored? That you are indeed created in the image of God? If we can learn this and take it to heart, it's the first step to living into a greater reality—a reality about ourselves that can give us the strength and courage to face our fears, our anxieties, our guilt, real and imagined.

On that frightening evening on the lake, my father and uncle guided our battered sailboat safely to the dock. Listening to the others who had been on board, I heard them talk of how frightened they were as well. But I also heard them talk of the exhilaration, the experience of sailing through the storm with their heads held up. But I missed that, having sat enclosed in the blackness of fear, afraid to move, afraid to look up, afraid to experience the storm. And I regretted giving in so totally to my fears.

Digging for Evil Treasure—Examining Our Fear

Exercise Five—Visual Prayer Using *Lectio Divina*

This particular exercise is adapted from the Benedictine prayer form called *lectio divina*, which has five steps or stages: silence (*silencio*), reading (*lectio*), meditation (*meditatio*), prayer (*oratio*), and contemplation (*contemplatio*). This form of prayer lends itself beautifully to the basic steps of visual prayer: We focus the heart in silence, reading and meditating; as we pray, our heart and focus on God, we perform *oratio*; and, finally, we contemplate by listening to the image.

Preparing and Focusing the heART

Prepare and organize your art materials.

Step One: *Silencio*

Close your eyes, take deep even breaths, and enter into a period of silence. Put everything aside and focus inward. Note your surroundings, the sounds, the thoughts in your mind. Breathe easily and deeply, accepting the world around you as it is at this moment. Next, focus on your body and note how it feels. Are you feeling any discomfort? Turn even further inward, focusing on your heart, noting how your heart feels. Can you imagine your heart in your mind's eye? Perhaps you can feel your heart beat. Is your heart feeling sad, anxious, stressed, contented? Note your inner feelings at this moment. As you begin to feel that you are in touch with yourself, open your heart and change your focus to God, and rest quietly in God's presence.

Step Two: *Lectio*

The readings for this particular prayer focus on fear. For future readings, you may use any passage of Scripture or reading you choose. When you're ready, read one of the following:

> Our deepest fear is not that we are inadequate. Our deepest fear is that we are powerful beyond measure. It is our light, not our darkness, that most frightens us. We ask ourselves. . . . "Who am I to be brilliant, gorgeous, talented and fabulous?" Who am I? You are a child of God; your playing small does not serve the world. There is nothing enlightened about shrinking, so that other people won't feel insecure around you. We are born to make manifest the glory of God within us. It is not just in some of us; it is in every one of us. And as we let our own light shine, we unconsciously give other people permission to do the same.[2]
>
> —Marianne Williamson

> My child, do not let these escape from your sight:
> keep sound wisdom and prudence,
> and they will be life for your soul
> and adornment for your neck.
> Then you will walk on you way securely
> and your foot will not stumble.
> If you sit down, you will not be afraid;

2. Marianne Williamson, *A Return to Love: Reflections on the Principles of a Course in Miracles* (New York: HarperCollins, 1992), 165.

> when you lie down, your sleep will be sweet.
> Do not be afraid of sudden panic,
> or of the storm that strikes the wicked;
> for the LORD will be your confidence
> and will keep your foot from being caught.
> —Proverbs 3:21–26

The purpose of *lectio divina* is to read something over and over until God speaks to you through it. Read your selection slowly several times, opening your heart to hear the voice of God. As you read with an open heart, you are listening for something that touches your deepest self, whether it's a single word or a phrase. Once you have focused on a word or phrase, write it down and move on to the next step.

Step Three: *Meditatio*

Consider the word or phrase carefully. Repeat it in your mind and your heart. Write down what goes through your mind when you repeat this phrase: memories, colors, feelings, images, ideas, people, etc. As you continue to open your heart and meditate on the phrase or word, one thing will stand out. This will be what God wants you to explore in a deeper way—it will be your prayer focus.

Prayer of the heART

Step Four: *Oratio*

At this step of *lectio divina*, you would normally create a prayer that expresses what's come out of your meditation. Since we're praying visually, you'll create with images instead of words.

Select the form of visual prayer to which you're led: expressive prayer, scribble prayer, or praying the mandala. At the top of the page, write the word or phrase that will be the focus of your prayer. As you pray your image, open your heart to what God reveals to you though the word or phrase. Remember, you are allowing God to draw the image *through* you, so don't try to control the choice of colors or images that appear. Allow the Holy Spirit to guide you.

Listening to the Image

Continue until you feel finished. Put your colors down and thank God for the gift of this image. Write down your first impression of what you have drawn. It may be a single word or a simple phrase.

Step Five: *Contemplatio*

On the page opposite the image you have drawn, reflect and dialogue with God in this time of written contemplation. Consider these basic questions to help in the dialogue process:

1. How do you feel when you look at the image? What is your initial impression of what you have drawn? What is your emotional reaction to the image, your mental acceptance of what you see, your physical response?
2. How do the colors you've used make you feel? What does each individual color symbolize for you? You can look into the universal symbolism of the colors to find a deeper understanding.
3. What does your image tell you about your fears? Were you already aware of them or are they new to you?
4. What does your dialogue with God tell you about yourself? What have you learned about God from this prayer?

Use any unanswered questions in ongoing prayers.

JOURNAL EXCERPT: CAROL'S PRAYER FOCUS: "GOD, HELP ME STOP BEING AFRAID OF THE PAST."

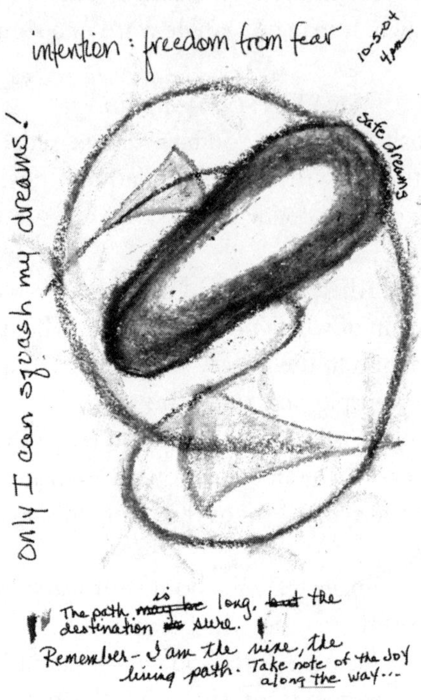

Fig. 17. Carol's meditation on fear.

"Freedom from fear. Safe dreaming. Only I can squash my dreams!

The path is long, the destination sure. Remember—I am the vine, the living path. Take note of the joy along the way. . . ."

9

— THE LIFE AND THE KINGDOM, THE LIGHT AND THE APOSTLES —

Gratitude

I have a particular necklace that I wear all the time with two connected Greek letters, Alpha and Omega, the first and last letters of the alphabet. This necklace is special to me because it was given to me by my grandmother. She used to wear it all the time before she became too sick, and she gave it to me before she moved into the nursing home. The Alpha and Omega symbolized hope for her, and reminded her to be thankful for all of life, even though it was very difficult. She buried two husbands. She nursed her first husband, my grandfather, who had tuberculosis, while simultaneously running a business and raising four daughters virtually by herself. She went through a lot of change, sadness, fear, and, I am sure, loneliness. Life was not easy for her.

"Remember, every cloud has a silver lining!" she always used to tell me when something upset me. I used to hate hearing it, especially when I was younger. Breaking up with boyfriends, having friends move away—those words were not comforting or encouraging. In fact, they made me think that my grandmother couldn't possibly understand what I was going through. Later, when I was in the midst of my divorce, I heard them again, and I'd hear them from her many times over the next eighteen years as I raised my daughters on my own. Slowly, I began to understand.

"Every cloud has a silver lining." My grandmother was not ignoring or denying the realities of this life or whatever difficult situation she referred to. It was not "cockeyed optimism" or "rose-colored glasses" but a reality, a truth that she carried deep within her heart. What she knew and what she was trying to teach me was the true meaning of hope, joy, and gratitude. Over her lifetime she had learned, and she taught me, that changes are never just endings; they are also beginnings, if you pay attention. "Every cloud has a silver lining" began to teach me that all of life, even and especially times of change and difficulty, brings with it new possibilities that can be seen as blessings and cause for gratitude.

Jesus said, "I am the Alpha and the Omega, the beginning and the end" (Rev 21:6). All beginnings signal an end of something and all endings bring with them new beginnings and new possibilities for gratitude to God and blessings within the unknown. I wear this necklace now and remember my grandmother and her life and all that she taught me about endings and possibilities. I wear this necklace now and remember to give thanks.

Living with hope. Living with the promise of a future with God. Living with the fullness of possibility. Living with thankfulness. Living hopefully is not always easy to do. Hope trusts that God is good, that God will fulfill God's promise to us. To have hope is to expect good. The writer of Ecclesiastes says, "whoever is joined with all the living has hope" (9:4). We're called to live in hope, to acknowledge the "silver lining" that allows us to live in expectation of our future and rejoice in our present in God.

Living with hope and thankfulness doesn't mean that life will get easier or that pain, violence, sadness, and disappointments will vanish. It means that we must change our attitude toward these things. We can choose a life of joy, of blessing, of thankfulness. Walter Burghardt said:

> You must be men and women of ceaseless hope, because only tomorrow can today's human and Christian promise be

> realized; and every tomorrow will have its own tomorrow, world without end. Every human act, every Christian act, is an act of hope. But that means you must be men and women of the present, you must live this moment—really live it, not just endure it—because this very moment, for all its imperfection and frustration, because of its imperfection and frustration, is pregnant with all sorts of possibilities, is pregnant with the future, is pregnant with love, is pregnant with Christ.[1]

Learning to give thanks, counting our blessings and living joyful lives, is a spiritual practice. Our thanksgiving, our gratitude is our pathway into the presence of God no matter what situation we find ourselves in. Living thankfully doesn't change the situation, or take away the horror or hurt. But as we give thanks, God opens our hearts to the knowledge of God's goodness and the fact that we are not alone.

It's easy to live with hope and joy when things are going well. It is easy to be grateful for the good things that happen in our lives. But to be thankful for all of our lives—the good and the bad, the moments of joy as well as the moments of sorrow, the successes and the failures, the rewards and the rejections—is hard work. When we divide our lives between good and bad, things we want to remember and things we want to forget, we rob ourselves of living into the fullness of who we are. God wants us to live with hope, joy, and thankfulness for the whole of our lives, and in doing so we experience the fullness of life, the fullness of ourselves, and the fullness of God. Paul says, "[B]e filled with the Spirit, as you sing psalms and hymns and spiritual songs among yourselves, singing and making melody to the Lord in your hearts, giving thanks to God the Father at all times and for everything in the name of our Lord Jesus Christ" (Ephesians 5:18b–20).

---

1. Walter Burghardt, *Sir, We Would Like to See Jesus: Homilies from a Hilltop* (New York: Paulist Press, 1982), 140.

Living the Life of Kingdom and Light

Exercise Six—Gratitude

Preparing and Focusing the heART

Prepare your sacred space and art materials. Center yourself, breathing deeply and slowly. Acknowledge how you are feeling mentally and physically. Let go of all the things on your mind and open your heart to God's presence within you. Enter into this period of meditation by focusing on your life, the good things and the bad.

For your prayer focus you may choose to do one of two things: simply thank God for your life, asking God to open your heart to blessings that you may not be aware of; or use this verse from Psalm 108 as your focus:

> My heart is steadfast, O God,
> My heart is steadfast;
> I will sing and make melody.
> Awake, my soul! (Psalm 108:1)

Continue this step of prayer until you feel ready to move on.

Prayer of the heART

At this time, choose a visual prayer technique, remembering to allow the Spirit to guide you both in the selection of colors and in what you draw. If you find yourself taking control of the exercise, re-center your focus and begin again. Continue praying your image until you feel finished.

Listening to the Image

Before you begin to dialogue, write the date and your prayer focus above your prayer image. You may want to consider the following questions as you dialogue:

1. What did you draw?
2. How does your image reflect thanksgiving to God or blessings in your life?
3. What can the colors, shapes, and images tell you about yourself and your life?

4. How did you feel when you were praying this image? How do you feel now? Is there a difference?
5. Has praying a prayer of thanksgiving helped you see blessings in your life that you had not realized before? Has it revealed anything about you? About God?
6. What do you think God wants you to take from this prayer time? Is it something you can apply to your life, and if so, will you do it? How?

JOURNAL EXCERPT: KELLY'S PRAYER FOCUS, "THANK YOU, GOD, FOR ALLAN'S NEW POSITION."

Fig. 18. Kelly's blessing.

"Renewal. Life is good. Allan never asks for much. He is so good. This mandala contains a seed being held by purple hands. The purple of transformation. God's hands. The seed is Allan and his new life. Our new life. It is red and has yellow and bright green flames coming from it. New growth. New possibilities. New opportunities for him. The blue and yellow rays point in toward the flames. They seem to come from God. I am thankful for Allan, for his love of God, for our chance to work together and share our ministry."

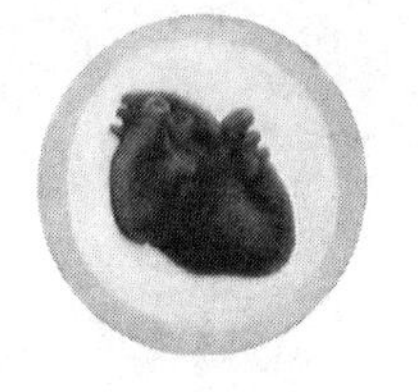

10

— HEAVENLY CITIES AND THE TREASURES OF GRACE; ALL THINGS ARE THERE —

Going Deeper—The Possibilities

One morning as I was doing the laundry, the phone rang. "Mom, hi." It was my daughter.

"Hi. What's going on?" I asked her, knowing that something was up by the tone of her voice and the time of day she was calling.

"Oh, nothing much. I'm on my way home from work." We talked for a few minutes and then she said she had something to run by me. She listed a few symptoms she was experiencing then asked, "Mom, do you think I may be pregnant?"

My mind whirled for a few minutes. I was excited at the thought of being a grandmother, but excitement gave way to shock. I was also concerned for my daughter because I knew that this wasn't a good time for her to begin a family. I reassured her as best I could and told her to wait and see, to try not to get too anxious about something so uncertain.

After she hung up, I tried to get back to work, folding clothes, matching socks, but my mind was racing with the memories of each of my daughters' births.

Sara was my first. I remember so well the night before she was born: I was in the hospital, scheduled to have a cesarean section the next morning at 7:00. I was so excited, I couldn't sleep. I kept thinking, "I'm going to have a baby! It's time! I'm having my baby!" I lay in the hospital bed for hours, thinking of all that was ahead, my stomach full of anxious butterflies. At some point, I became aware of a bright light coming through my window. I got up, waddled over, and there was the full moon, bright and benevolent, like a blessing from God on me and my child. I stood there, bathed in God's presence, filled with a sense of grace and hope and the fullness of life's possibilities. I don't know how long I stood there, but I finally went back to bed and fell asleep. The next morning, I had a beautiful baby girl.

Emily was next. Sara had just turned two and was very active, and I was very tired. Tired, but excited. The first night after she was born was difficult as she slept in the crib beside my bed. The C-section was harder on me this time; it hurt whenever I had to pick her up to feed or change her.

The night was dark and still, and I was finally sleeping. Emily's cries woke me and I leaned over, took her in my arms, and placed her at my breast. As she nursed, I remember holding her tiny, perfect little hand and exploring each tiny finger as it curled and uncurled, trying to grasp hold. I was too tired to put her back in the crib when she was finished, so I centered her on my chest and securely tucked the sheets around her, and we both fell asleep. And that's how Emily spent her first night.

It turns out my daughter wasn't pregnant after all, and I must admit I was a little disappointed. But the possibility of new life evoked memories that are so important to me. I held on to these memories when the girls were going through so much pain and difficulty in high school, and they helped me get through the tough times. The memories and hopes were back now, flowing over me and filling me with a sense of awe at the workings of creation and the immense depth of the heart.

I'm constantly amazed at how much the heart can hold. I truly thought that I couldn't love anyone as much as I loved my two girls. Then, after eighteen years of being a single mom, I met my husband and his children and reached another level of love. And with the prospect of a grandchild, my heart was ready for even more, ready for the next exponential leap of love and experience of life.

Continuing the Process

Life is constantly amazing me. Each day brings with it the opportunity to discover more about myself, my heart, my God. Whether it is memories I haven't thought of for years, or the realization of my blessings. Whether it is frustration, or sadness, or just trying to muddle through the chaos a day may bring. Each day offers the opportunity to travel a little further into the realm of the heart.

Just as each day offers opportunities for stepping closer to God, so too does the ongoing practice of visual prayer. As you continue the process, opening your heart and letting God speak to your life experiences through images, you will find yourself amazed by the discoveries you will find. By incorporating visual prayer into your regular prayer discipline, you'll discover new dimensions about yourself and God. Layer upon layer of life experiences will surface, allowing you to reflect upon and dialogue with God about the things going on in your life. This time is sacramental—it is a time when you are intimately involved in the outward and visible sign of God's inward and spiritual grace.

Marion, a woman in one of my visual prayer groups, shared with me what visual prayer has meant to her: "[It has] added such an incredibly important dimension to my spiritual life, indeed, to my life as a whole. Through practicing visual journaling, I have been led to explore art in other areas of my life. I am really enjoying trying to develop my creative 'eye' and skills which I had long assumed were nonexistent! It is a slow process, of course, but a very satisfying and enjoyable one and feels very much like God is calling me to explore art as a whole new dimension that will assist me in moving toward what God created me to be. . . . I cannot actually find words to express the difference it has made and continues to make in my relationship with God and in my personal healing."

As you continue this journey towards God, traveling deeper and deeper into your heart, discovering and exploring all kinds of memories, feelings, and experiences, you may desire someone to share your experiences with. I encourage this. In working with my visual prayer spiritual direction groups, I've found that sharing visual images with others helps me gain deeper insight into what God is revealing. Others see things that you may have missed, and with time, each member of the group begins to understand the visual language of other members. In this type of group, it is important to make a covenant with each other that includes the following guidelines:

- Each member of the group will practice visual prayer and journal on a regular basis.
- No one will be forced to share their visual prayers.
- A member can decline to receive feedback from the others.
- Feedback should only be offered as possible insight only, not as truth.
- The group session is intended for sharing spiritual insight, not personal therapy. Members should seek a priest, spiritual director, or therapist if an issue exceeds the bounds of spiritual insight.

Exploring the Possibilities

When my heart offers me an opportunity for discovery, like the memories of my daughters' births, I find that I love to explore all that the experience offers, good or bad—gaining insight into myself and how God is present is that experience. As you continue the process of visual prayer and go deeper into the possibilities it offers, you will find yourself wanting to know more—wanting to be able to read deeper into the images God is giving you. As I have said before, there are many levels of insight that can be gained from visual prayer. Some days you may find that the process of visual prayer, the time spent intentionally with God, is enough and no journaling is necessary. Other times, simply reflecting on the image and looking at your immediate response and the colors is enough. There will also be times when you'll want to explore the symbolism of your prayer image much further.

I've presented various methods of deciphering the color symbolism in your prayers. And although color is one of the primary ways the Spirit speaks to us, there are other visual symbols you can explore. Looking at the symbolic meanings of realistic images such as trees, animals, flowers, birds, water, and the sun can bring a deeper understanding of what God is revealing to you. Shapes are also important: spirals, circles, squares, and triangles all carry specific symbolic meaning.

If you are interested in looking deeper into the symbolism of colors and images, there are several books I recommend. Susanne F. Fincher's *Creating Mandalas for Insight, Healing, and Self-Expression* (Boston: Shambhala Publications, 1991), is thorough, clear, and easy to understand. Two other books I use regularly are J. E. Cirlot's *A Dictionary of Symbols*, 2nd ed., (New York: Dover Publications, 2002), and George Ferguson's *Signs & Symbols in Christian Art* (New York: Oxford University Press, 1961).

The Depths of the heART

Our lives are constantly changing. We go though periods when things are good and stable (the innocence of my childhood, the joy of my two daughters' births), as well as periods when we're faced with trials, pain, and chaos (the pain of divorce). I remember the little fears, the big fears, the doubts when faced with change, and the sense frustration in challenging relationships. I'm thankful for my husband, our five daughters, son-in-law, and two grandsons, and the fullness of our family. I'm ready for whatever ups and downs come our way.

Visual prayer is a way for me to process with God the events and experiences of my life. It's a form of prayer that lends itself to the changes life brings. There are times when I use visual prayer every day, and times when I step away from it for a while. But I always return.

As Macarius says, the heart is a small vessel, but it is deep and holds many things. There is never a time when we will have fully explored the depth and breadth of the landscape of our hearts. Just when we think we have examined every rough road, every precipice, every poisonous beast that could possibly be hidden there, we will find more, or life will add more. Conversely, when we think we've explored every aspect of God, the angels, the treasures of grace, the love in our hearts, we will find more, or life will give us more to see, more to experience.

God has given us great gifts: the gift of our life journey, the gift of sight and insight, the gift of heart, the gift of love. Travel your life well. Open your heart to God.

Thanks be to God.

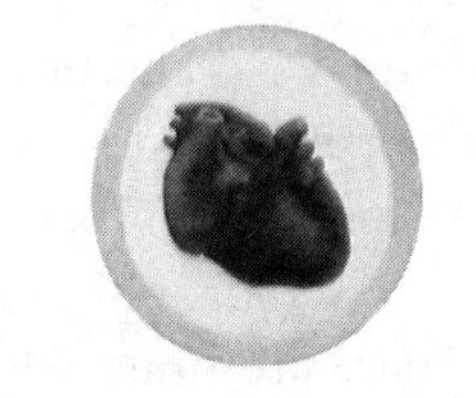

APPENDIX
Color Symbolism

As an artist and former art teacher, I've discovered the deep significance of color both in my own work and in the work of my students. Color can express thoughts, feelings, and even physical sensations. Understanding the symbolic meaning of the colors you have used in your visual prayer images can lead you to a deeper meaning in the message presented. Some colors are obvious and easy to understand. Some will be more difficult. As you'll see, most colors have different meanings depending on shade; for instance, powder blue has a different meaning than midnight blue.

We each have our own color preferences and associations with particular colors: what a color symbolizes for us is not necessarily related to our like or dislike of that color. It's important to pay attention to these personal associations with colors first when listening to your image. It's also helpful and enlightening to look at the universal, cultural, and traditional symbolic associations of each color. Understanding these associations can open up new possibilities, new areas of insight, and perhaps new questions. In the following color descriptions, see if something jumps out at or resonates with you, and explore how that color relates to you and your prayer image.

The following color chart includes some of the main symbolism of basic colors.[1]

---

1. In compiling the color information used in the appendix, I have used several sources, one of which is a series of "Color Handouts" I used when I taught high school art. I have also used several books on symbolism in addition to Susanne Fincher's excellent book on mandalas, which I highly recommend (see Bibliography for more information). As all of the color meanings I have used are included in some form in all of these sources, I have not made specific reference to any particular book. I encourage you to look at these for more detailed information.

Black

- death, the unconscious, mystery, darkness, emptiness, sickness
- the womb, the place of new beginnings
- the period preceding understanding or spiritual enlightenment
- important changes or life transitions that cannot yet be seen
- sadness, anger, fear, remorse, mourning, depression, loss, "black mood"

Blue

- Blue and Light Blue: clear skies, calm waters, cool shadows, cold

    - peace, calmness, stability, truth, serenity
    - spirit, the heavenly, inspiration, clear thinking, religious feelings
    - God the Father, the Virgin Mary, heavenly love
    - compassion, loyalty, unfailing love
    - as water: cool, cleansing, refreshing, nourishing, baptism
    - as mother: nurturing, compassionate, unconditional

- Dark Blue or Indigo is similar to black: night sky, stormy weather or seas, inner darkness, unconscious, depression, loss, sleep, life-threatening, the awakening of intuition, psychological rebirth; as mother: devouring, impersonal, overbearing

Brown

- earth, fertility, possibility of new beginnings
- barren, empty field, loss, sorrow, penitence
- home, comfort, stability, simplicity
- "down to earth," trustworthy
- as excrement: low self-esteem and feelings of worthlessness or, like manure, can be transforming
- end of a life cycle

- blocked energy, low opinion of self, need for security
- spiritual death, degradation

Gold

- sun, illumination, divine light, state of glory

Green

- nature, environment, healthy, renewal, youthful vigor, spring
- generosity, fertility, harmony, free spirit
- presence of God in earthly things
- healing: power of life to create, heal, and renew
- dark green: envy, jealousy, misfortune, venom, rotting vegetation, decay

Gray

- security, reliability, modest, mature, solid, conservative, practical, wisdom
- old age, sadness, boring, depression, indifference
- neutral, stone, ashes, mist
- atonement, humility, mourning

Magenta

- bold, dramatic, individualistic, excitement, restless, or freeing energy
- motivation, readiness to step out into something new, taking action, voicing opinions
- feminine strength
- impatient, strong ego, loss of focus, excessive emotion

Maroon

- old wounds
- an item or issue you need to examine

Orange

- energy, balance, warmth, enthusiasm, nervous, vibrant, demanding attention

- pride, ambition, egoism, cruelty, outcast, or criminal
- strong sense of identity, healthy assertiveness, striving
- fire, purification, deepening of spiritual understanding through trial, misfortune, rejection
- lack of self-discipline, inappropriate use of power, hostility toward those in authority

Peach

- soft, juicy, full
- pleasure, sensuality, mature sexuality
- feminine ability to create life
- inner feminine energy
- overly romantic, sexually indulgent

Pink

- flesh, sensuality, material
- emotions, innocence
- feminine, inner child
- physical pleasures and pains, physical health, illness, or stress
- love

Purple/Violet

- color of gods, royalty, power, pride, justice, truth, not ordinary
- cruelty, arrogance
- passion, suffering, penitence, mystical union
- transformation, process of personal growth
- need for support or need to attract attention, self-centered

Lavender

- virtue, spiritual awakening or insight, desire to escape reality, distrust

Red

- excitement, energy, passion, willpower, desire, speed
- strength, power, heat, aggression
- love and hate

- danger, fire, blood, violence, aggression, intensity
- sign of life, healing, sacrifice, atonement, process of becoming whole
- Holy Spirit
- will to thrive, commitment to life, acceptance of the physical body
- life force, lust, fertility

Turquoise

- healing: physical, spiritual, and psychological
- need to distance self from painful or difficult events that threaten the ability to cope
- need to have closure with past
- motherly nurturing directed toward self, care for oneself

White

- reverence, purity, simplicity, peace, humility, redemption, mystical illumination, ecstasy, joy, light, life, creation, timelessness, healing
- innocence, youth, birth
- readiness for change, hidden area of intense emotion
- daylight, clarity, order
- winter, snow, good
- cold, clinical, sterile, clean
- nothingness, death, ashes, bone

Yellow

- joy, happiness, optimism, idealism, imagination, hope
- sunshine, summer, divinity, truth, life-giving power
- intellect, generosity, ability to see and understand
- self-awareness, individuality, new chapter in life
- need for a release from conflict, seeking, developing
- need for change or balance
- dishonesty, cowardice, betrayal, deceit, illness, hazard
- jealousy, degradation, contagion

— BIBLIOGRAPHY —

Allen, Pat B. *Art Is a Way of Knowing*. Boston: Shambala Publications, 1995.

Auden, W. H. *He Is the Way*. New York: Church Hymnal Corporation, 1982.

Brother Lawrence. *The Practice of the Presence of God.*

Burghardt, Walter. *Sir, We Would Like to See Jesus: Homilies from a Hilltop*. New York: Paulist Press, 1982.

Cirlot, J. E. *A Dictionary of Symbols*. 2nd ed. New York: Dover Publications, 2002.

Farrelly-Hansen, Mimi, ed. *Spirituality and Art Therapy*. New York: Jessica Kingsley, 2001.

Ferguson, George. *Signs & Symbols in Christian Art*. New York: Oxford University Press, 1961.

Fincher, Susanne F. *Creating Mandalas for Insight, Healing, and Self-Expression*. Boston: Shambhala Publications, 1991.

Ganim, Barbara, and Susan Fox. *Visual Journaling: Going Deeper than Words*. Wheaton, Ill.: Quest Books, 1999.

Godwin, Gail. Heart: *A Natural History of the Heart-Filled Life*. New York: Perennial, 2002.

Horovitz, Ellen G. *Spiritual Art Therapy: An Alternative Path*. 2nd ed. Springfield, Ill.: Charles D. Thomas, 2002.

The Hymnal 1982. New York: Church Hymnal Corporation, 1982.

The Inside Story: Understanding the Power of Feelings. Boulder Creek, Calif.: Institute of HeartMath, 2002. Available online at http://www.heartmathstore.com.

The Interpreter's Dictionary of the Bible, Vol. E–F. New York: Abingdon Press, 1962.

Jung, Carl. *Man and His Symbols*. New York: Dell, 1968.

Keating, Thomas. *Foundations for Centering Prayer*. New York: Continuum, 2002.

MacDonald, George. *Lilith*. Grand Rapids, Mich.: Eerdmans, 1981.

———. *The Shopkeeper's Daughter*. Wheaton Ill.: Victor Books, 1986.

Maloney, George A., S.J., ed. *Pseudo-Macarius: The Fifty Spiritual Homilies and The Great Letter*. New York: Paulist Press, 1992.

Meister Eckhardt, *Breakthrough: Meister Eckhart's Creation Spirituality in New Translation*. Introduction and Commentaries by Matthew Fox. New York: Doubleday, 1980.

Rilke, Rainer Maria. "Turning," in *Uncollected Poems: Rainer Maria Rilke*. Edward Snow, ed. New York: North Point Press, 1996.

Sewell, Marilyn, ed. *Cries of the Spirit*. Boston: Beacon Press, 1991.

Smith, Martin. *The Word Is Very Near You*. Cambridge, Mass.: Cowley, 1989.

Webster's New Twentieth Century Dictionary Unabridged. 2nd ed. New York: Simon and Schuster, 1972.

Williamson, Marianne. *A Return to Love : Reflections on the Principles of a Course in Miracles*. New York: HarperCollins, 1992.